Disabled people and employment

A review of research and development work

Helen Barnes, Patricia Thornton and Sue Maynard Campbell

First published in Great Britain in 1998 by

The Policy Press
University of Bristol
Fourth Floor, Beacon House
Queen's Road
Bristol BS8 1QU
UK

Tel no   +44 (0)117 331 4054
Fax no   +44 (0)117 331 4093
E-mail   tpp-info@bristol.ac.uk
www.policypress.org.uk

In association with the Joseph Rowntree Foundation

© The Policy Press and the Joseph Rowntree Foundation, 1998

Transferred to Digital Print 2006

ISBN 1 86134 121 0

Helen Barnes was formerly a research fellow at the Social Policy Research Unit, University of York, **Patricia Thornton** is a research fellow at the Social Plicy Research Unit, University of York and **Sue Maynard Campbell** is Director of Equal Ability.

The **Joseph Rowntree Foundation** has supported this project as part of its programme of research and innovative development projects, which it hopes will be of value to policy makers and practitioners. The facts presented and the views expressed in this report, however, are those of the authors and not necessarily those of the Foundation.

Cover design by Qube Design Associates, Bristol.
Printed in Great Britain by Marston Book Services, Oxford.

Contents

List of abbreviations

ABAPSTAS	Association of Blind and Partially Sighted Teachers and Students
ACENVO	Association of Chief Executives of Voluntary Organisations
ASBAH	Association for Spina Bifida and Hydrocephalus
AtW	Access to Work
CVS	Council for Voluntary Service
DDA	1995 Disability Discrimination Act
DEA	Disabled Employment Advisors
DfEE	Department for Education and Employment
DIAL	Disability Information and Advice Line
DoH	Department of Health
DRUL	Disability Research Unit, Leeds
DSS	Department of Social Security
EFD	Employers' Forum for Disability
ES	Employment Service
FYD	Friends for the Young Deaf
GLAD	Greater London Association of Disabled People
IT	information technology
JRF	Joseph Rowntree Foundation
LFS	Labour Force Survey
NOP	National Opinion Poll
OPCS	Office of Population and Censuses and Surveys
OSCA	Outcomes of social care for adults
PACTs	Placement Advisory and Counselling Teams
PSI	Policy Studies Institute
RADAR	Royal Association for Disability and Rehabilitation
RNIB	Royal National Institute for the Blind
TECs	Training and Enterprise Councils
TUC	Trades Union Congress

Introduction

Part One of the report explains why this review was carried out and what it covers, set in the context of a highly dynamic environment influenced not only by structural changes in the labour market, but also by rapidly changing policy initiatives.

Part Two considers research to date and existing research and development initiatives as they relate to different stages in the career path of a disabled person, identifying gaps in what has been covered, and priorities for further work.

Part Three of the review draws together the themes and evaluates the prospects for future research and development in the areas which have been identified as a priority by disabled people themselves.

Part One
Setting the scene

About the review

The Joseph Rowntree Foundation (JRF) is a major funder of research and development work, with a strong commitment to effecting change through research with the involvement of disabled people. The Foundation commissioned this review as part of its programme of work on 'Independence and Quality of Life'. The aim is to help JRF set priorities for future work it might support relating to disabled people and the barriers encountered in obtaining, maintaining or advancing in employment.

What the review set out to do

We set out to do three things:

1. To assess past and current research and ask:

- what has been researched and why?

- how has research taken account of disabled people's perspectives?

- what are its limitations and what are the priorities for further research?

2. To review practical programmes and initiatives and ask:

- what is happening on the ground and why?

- how should we evaluate projects aiming to promote employment prospects for disabled people?

- where are the gaps and what are the priorities for development?

3. To develop an agenda for research and development work and ask:

- how should the research identified as necessary be done?

- who needs to be involved, and how, if research and development work is to result in change?

What the review covered

Research and development work relating to disabled people and employment is a big topic. Our focus was on accessing work and issues within the workplace for disabled people. Many within the disabled people's movement argue that it is not possible to tackle employment in isolation and that until disabled people have access to adequate housing, support, education and transport they are bound to be at a disadvantage in gaining employment. JRF expected that the review would recognise this view, without detracting from its primary focus. Recent work for the Foundation (Kestenbaum, 1996) has comprehensively reviewed research on appropriate housing, personal assistance, transport and a range of access issues, in the context of Independent Living. An earlier research-based commentary, also supported by JRF and conducted by the British Council of Organisations of Disabled People (Barnes, 1991) had examined education, disability benefits, the physical environment and leisure, as well as employment, from the perspective of institutional discrimination against disabled people.

Research on the impact of the social security benefits system was not sought explicitly because the Foundation had recently commissioned a review of disabled people, work and benefits research (Thornton and Lunt, 1996). Concerns about the barriers to paid work created by the benefits system nevertheless permeated the review. The growing literature on supported employment is not covered extensively, given another forthcoming JRF review (Simons, 1998).

Coverage was limited to Great Britain and (apart from some basic texts) the review covers recent literature only. No formal constraints were placed on the types of literature sought, but the review concentrated on research into the disabled person's experience; indeed, the inclusion of the disabled person's perspective is a yardstick for research.

Our approach was guided by the social model of disability (see Oliver, 1990; Barnes, 1991), which acknowledged that people are disabled by the physical, organisational and attitudinal barriers within society, rather than by their impairment or medical condition. As a result we made it clear that we were interested in the experiences of anyone with, or with a history of, a physical or sensory impairment, or a particular medical condition, who encounters barriers or discrimination in obtaining employment or staying in work. We specifically included those who have experienced mental illness, have learning difficulties/disability, or have HIV and Aids. Disability is not the only dimension affecting work; the divisions of class, gender, 'race' and age interact with one another and with disability. We have tried, wherever possible, to identify such interactions.

In the course of the review we tried to identify common ground among disabled people who encounter barriers relating to employment. We were thinking of issues which cut across impairment, such as the needs of disabled women returners, the needs of those who have never had employment, or those who have been highly trained in work which is no longer appropriate for them because of an impairment. In this aim we had limited success: most interests, whether in disability organisations, research or projects on the ground, relate to specific impairments. This 'mind set' is widespread, perpetuated by funding structures

and the interest of impairment-related membership organisations and lobby groups in serving their constituents.

How the review was carried out

There were three elements to the review: consultation; a review of research; and identification of development projects.

Broad-based consultation

Our starting point was that disabled people's views and experiences of the barriers in employment, and ideas about what needed to be looked at, would shape the research and development agenda. Reviewing the research literature and projects on the ground would then help us to see whether what has been done so far matches up to what disabled people say is needed. But because we wanted to produce an agenda for change, not merely to list the difficulties which need to be explored and understood, and because we recognised that employers, service providers and other workers could have different views of what needs to be done, we extended our consultation to the other 'stakeholders'.

Unusually for a research review, a lot of time and effort was put into consultation – with disabled people, disabled people's organisations and other organisations with disability interests, as well as with researchers in the field. The consultation served a double purpose, as people were not only asked for ideas on what should be looked at but also were invited to tell us about research and projects.

A covering letter and response form (4,350 in all) were included in the mailings of seven national organisations; they were also made available to people attending five disability and employment conferences or seminars. We also wrote to or telephoned people active in research or in projects we knew about and circulated notices on three e-mail lists; and some organisations copied information among their own members or staff, or collated views at meetings or conferences.

At the start of the review process we invited people from organisations of and for disabled people to take part in either one of two telephone conferences or in face-to-face discussions with a member of the team. One-to-one telephone discussions were also arranged where the other options were not possible.

Towards the end of the first exploratory phase, early findings were presented to and discussed at a specially convened forum of 20 disabled people attending the Association of Disabled Professionals' Conference 'Positive about Employment'. Many further ideas emerged there.

Finally, a preliminary agenda for research and development was discussed with a range of stakeholders at a specially arranged seminar.

Identifying the research

In addition to the usual searches for published research, the team approached researchers and the main commissioning and grant-giving bodies, known to be active in this area, with the particular aim of finding research in progress. People who responded to the call for ideas and information helped to locate useful studies available locally, including work by PhD students. Useful databases included the *Directory of disability information sources* (DSS, 1997).

Mapping development projects

We had planned to map practical initiatives in England, Wales and Scotland. This turned out to be over-ambitious, both because of the huge number of projects in the field and because of the scarcity o f published overviews. A new report by Maynard Campbell and Smyth will partly fill the gap in descriptive information about local projects (1998).

We discovered an unquantifiable number of projects, often locally funded and accountable to

a range of funding bodies, operating in isolation from one another. Information within the remit of national or European grant-giving programmes can be little more than lists of projects or, in one case, merely a list of grant recipients which gave no information about project objectives. Published evaluations to date concentrate more on the processes of putting the programme into operation and its overall effectiveness than on describing the aims, content and effectiveness of specific projects.

For more detailed information, we relied on people involved in projects bringing them to our attention and providing reports. Otherwise, the main sources were the small number of directories and practice guides, often focusing on one of the better known types of provision such as social firms, mental health projects or supported employment projects and affirming them as good practice (see, for example, Grove et al, 1997; Pozner et al, 1996). Accordingly, we can give only a broad picture of development projects and comment generally on 'good practice' and on where priorities might rest. We have highlighted some particularly innovative projects in Part Two of this review. A fully comprehensive information resource for people seeking to develop practice is recommended.

Acknowledging ideas

The people we consulted shared their work in progress, experiences and ideas for the future agenda willingly and openly, often reflecting a personal or organisational commitment to improving disabled people's employment through research and development. Those ideas provide the mainstay of this report, from which the rest of its fabric hangs. All unattributed quotes are from disabled people who took part in this review (Part Two includes quotes from non-disabled people). In the appendix we have tried to acknowledge by name everyone who contributed to the review.

2

The review in context

National developments

The review was conducted from September 1997 to February 1998, a period when employment prospects for disabled people became a 'hot topic'. New development initiatives such as the National Disability Development Initiative were launched. The new round of HORIZON projects, within the EMPLOYMENT Community Initiative of the European Social Funds, came on stream and the government consulted on its New Deal programme for people with a disability or long-term illness and announced the first call for innovative projects. At the policy level, a task force was set up to review aspects of the 1995 Disability Discrimination Act (DDA) and a consultation on the exclusion of small firms from the Act was announced. Not least, there was considerable speculation and activity during this period over the new government's possible plans for disability benefit reform. A steady stream of consultative meetings, conferences and seminars on disability and employment brought together policy makers, disabled people's organisations (both campaigning and providing groups), other provider organisations, employers, trades unionists and researchers. The resurgence of interest in the area, initially stimulated by the introduction of disability discrimination legislation, has led to a new wave of research and practice-based publications.

In recent years, new players have entered the national stage. Employing organisations, and trades unionists, have articulated their own interests in advancing employment opportunities for disabled people. The Employers' Forum for Disability (EFD), a membership organisation of mainly large public and private corporations, and the Trades Union Congress (TUC) have been active in trying to effect change within organisations, as well as lobbying at national level. The EFD argues that employers, as well as disabled people, have needs which must be addressed by national policy; employers are also customers of publicly-provided services such as the Disability Service (Schneider-Ross, 1995). Both the TUC and national employers' organisations advocate the 'business case' for representation of disabled people in the workforce. Regional and local employers' networks are encouraged by government (DfEE, 1997).

At the same time, national voluntary organisations, which have traditionally provided residential, therapeutic or care services for disabled people, have expanded into services to promote the transition to employment, and many new charitable organisations work specifically in the employment field, some in partnership with employers and their organisations. Some national organisations, notably the Royal National Institute for the Blind (RNIB), have also begun to work with employers to help people who become disabled to retain employment. Organisations of disabled people have moved into a service-providing role in the area of employment, and a number of small businesses run by disabled people offer consultancy and training to employing organisations and to disabled people.

Local activity

At local level the picture fragments into an unquantifiable number of uncoordinated employment projects for disabled people, many tailored for those with learning difficulties or mental health problems. The situation is made more complex by the growth of private and voluntary services, sometimes funded from their own resources but more usually dependent on piecemeal funding from national and local statutory and charitable sources and European funding programmes. National policy requires the disability services of the Employment Service (ES) and the employer-led Training and Enterprise Councils (TECs) to contract rehabilitation and training services to independent agencies. Questions have been raised about how to evaluate the effectiveness of such large numbers of independent providers.

Coordination of local activity is a major problem. No single authority has responsibility for services to promote employment of disabled people. Local authorities have responsibility for community care but needs assessment and care management are conceived as social care functions and rarely include employment among the range of 'needs'. One local authority survey which did ask about these issues found that only 29% of community care service users had paid work; over 60% expressed an interest in employment or training (Kingston JCAG, 1997). Health authorities have traditionally been reluctant to recognise the therapeutic benefits of work, although partnerships with voluntary organisations, notably in the mental health field, are beginning to change attitudes. Coordination between health and social care authorities, despite cost-shunting tendencies, is relatively good compared with their relations either with locally-based offices of the ES or with TECs. Connecting employment support services to social services departments and health authorities may help to promote user-involvement in service design and evaluation, a concept which seems alien within the national ES (Hyde, 1996).

Individual local efforts seem to be fairly responsive to individual need, and the importance of employment in supporting disabled people's independence and quality of life is beginning to be recognised in practice. However, Shepherd (1997) notes that there are very few examples of a coordinated range of opportunities which would offer disabled people a number of different options, geared to different abilities and aspirations.

A high proportion of projects are impairment specific, notably under the HORIZON initiative, partly because sources of additional funding are linked to particular impairments and very few address pan-disability issues. Despite a commitment to innovation, of the 635 HORIZON projects across the European Union which came to an end in 1997, only one was concerned with new working patterns and only 22 with new types of work; in addition, despite the particular problems they experience in the labour market, only 2% of projects were aimed specifically at women (European Commission, 1997).

The state of research

Policy-led research

Much of the research literature on the employment situation of disabled people is policy-led, most commissioned by the Department for Education and Employment (DfEE) and by the ES (an agency of the DfEE). Their evaluation studies have looked mainly at the effectiveness of particular policies (such as supported employment or policies to change recruitment and retention practices) or at particular services and schemes (such as Placement Advisory and Counselling Teams [PACTs], the Access to Work programme [AtW] or the Job Introduction Scheme) which aim to increase the representation of disabled people in employment. The broad objectives of policies are already set and the purpose of research is to assess how far they are being met. While policy-led research may seek the views of the users (disabled people and employers) to tailor policies and services more closely to generalised need within the population group, the *individual* experience of services is rarely sought (the qualitative research commissioned from Social and Community Planning Research (Thomas, 1992) is exceptional).

These 'top-down' studies have also tended to look at policies in isolation from one another, making it difficult to see the system as a whole. Similarly, disabled people's views, when asked, are captured at a single point in the system (as a user of AtW, for example) and the overall picture of the 'job-seeker's journey', as advocated by the EFD, is not obtained.

Reactive research

There is also some research, mostly supported by non-governmental bodies, which operates within the existing employment policy and service framework but looks at effects on consumers. Here, the aim is to influence the way these policies and services are put into practice so that they are more effective in providing what disabled people need and want. Much of this research follows the official ways of demarcating services (for example, by looking at disabled people's experiences of using services under the remit of ES disability services) and much of it is concerned with particular impairment groups; for example, the impact of legislation on people with epilepsy (Delany, work in progress), or the experience of the AtW programme for people with visual impairment (RNIB/RADAR, 1995). A small body of independent research has asked disabled people about policies they would prefer as well as their experiences of existing policies (Cunningham, 1993; Hyde and Howes, 1993).

There is a body of research in the fields of industrial relations, employment law, personnel management and occupational health, rarely acknowledged in reviews of this kind, which looks at the fit between employers' requirements and public policy in the field of disability. The DDA is beginning to have a positive effect in integrating social policy research on the impact of national policies on disabled people with research which takes the firm as its starting point. However, research in the latter field, looking, for example, at equal opportunity policies or the management of disability in the workplace, rarely examines the impact of enterprise policies and practices on disabled employees. In our consultations, disabled people questioned the real impact of enterprise 'paper policies' on people who were intended to benefit from them.

Disability as an equal opportunities issue

One drawback in reviewing literature on 'disabled people and employment' is that studies where disability is not the sole focus can be overlooked. But the absence of research, other than population surveys, which looks at how disabled people fare outside special programmes is striking – a criticism raised by a number of people consulted.

One of the issues that disabled people have raised is that much 'special' research is done 'about' them, but that their perspective, as part of the workforce or potential workforce, among other things, is not taken into account in setting up mainstream research projects. They argue that in many research projects disability could and should be addressed within an equal opportunities framework, rather than being relegated to a 'special needs' category. The structure of research funding may unwittingly perpetuate the exclusion of disabled people from the mainstream. Funding for disability research is often separate from other programmes, with the result that a programme on work may exclude the experiences of disabled people, while research into employment will often not be an obvious choice for funding bodies traditionally concerned with social and community care.

Disabled people from minority ethnic groups

Disabled people from minority ethnic groups may face additional discrimination. In using services overall, awareness of what is available is lower among black and minority ethnic groups than for the white population, take-up levels are reduced and there is a widespread view that services which are provided are unwelcoming or unsuitable (CVS/GLAD,1997). This is equally likely to be true of employment services for disabled people. Specific issues include language barriers, racist attitudes among providers and inappropriate services. As many employers do not monitor the employment of people from ethnic minorities, they tend to be invisible. The interaction between race, disability and gender is complex, and the multiple oppression of disabled women from minority ethnic groups is rarely addressed by research (Vernon, 1997).

Our review found very few organisations working specifically on employment issues for disabled people from minority ethnic communities. For instance, a directory of projects for Deaf people from black and ethnic minority groups (Darr et al, 1997) found only one or two which had any brief for employment issues; the vast majority were concerned with improving the level and quality of health and other services provided. Several reasons for this were suggested to us by those we did manage to contact. These included lack of resources to work on these issues; the fact that minority ethnic populations as a whole were experiencing high levels of unemployment and therefore the prospects for disabled people from these communities – regardless of the efforts made to assist them – were seen as very limited indeed. In some cases, the role played by a disabled person within the family was seen as being of greater value than the possibility of their working.

Project evaluation

Just how many of the multitude of local projects are subject to research-based evaluation is not known. However, evidence would seem to indicate 'not many'. Those on the ground appear to be trying hard just to keep going and find sources of funding to enable projects to continue. Any efforts to look at quality and effectiveness from the recipient's perspective are few and far between, and there is little evidence of attempts to evaluate projects in a wider context. The involvement of disabled people in the establishment or evaluation of research and development initiatives is even rarer. Even large and established research funders do not always specify the involvement of disabled people in research as a criterion for selection. An evaluation of the 78 UK organisations which participated in the HELIOS II programme (Bolderson et al, 1997) found that most of the organisations which successfully applied for funding were those which had prior experience of European Commission funding initiatives and networks, rather than those which had been most effective in involving disabled people in their establishment and evaluation.

Many evaluations revolve round 'through-put' to satisfy funders. Walsh et al (1997) report on the mid-term evaluation of NOW, HORIZON and YOUTHSTART projects in Great Britain, within the European Commission's EMPLOYMENT programme. Overall, conventional outcome measures were considered inadequate; qualitative outcomes were thought to be more relevant. For instance, a number of projects said that they were concerned with the quality of work experience and training rather than labour market outcomes, recognising that these

were a long-term measure, beyond the life of particular initiatives.

A key priority of the HELIOS programme was to publish a guide to good practice in equal opportunities for disabled people. This document stresses the role of work as something which integrates an individual in society, and promotes the right of disabled people to employment, in addition to providing examples of good practice from across the European Union (European Commission, 1996).

There seem to be relatively few arrangements with the major funding programmes for cross-project evaluation, although individual projects can be required to have some evaluation in place. The emphasis on innovation as an eligibility criterion was thought unhelpful.

> "There are lots of small innovative projects out there, but we are not learning lessons and moving on from them. We should not end up with a situation where thousands of other 'innovative' projects get funded. How can funding be directed to effect real change?"

Employment, research and the disabled people's movement

The employment situation of disabled people has received comparatively little attention from writers in the disability movement (Thornton and Lunt, 1995; Hyde, 1996), with the exception of the comprehensive work on institutional discrimination (Barnes, 1991). One explanation is that the first priority for the movement, given its links with the Independent Living movement, lay with removing barriers to the 'primary needs' (housing, personal assistance, transport and so on) which, if satisfied, would maximise access to mainstream opportunities such as employment. Whether work is a 'primary need' in the Independent Living context has seldom been discussed.

Jahoda (1982) suggests that employment fulfils a number of important functions. It provides an enforced pattern of activity and creates a time structure to the day; it is a source of social contacts outside the household, and gives people the sense of participating in a wider collective purpose; and it provides the individual with social status and a sense of identity. Jahoda's argument that in advanced capitalist societies needs for life structure and ties with the community can only be met through employment does not, however, adequately address the potential differences between men's and women's experiences (Arber, 1991; Vernon, 1996; 1997), nor the effects for those who seek to fulfil such roles in ways other than employment. PhD research currently being carried out at Plymouth University considers class and gender differences in the integration of disabled people into work, on the basis of interviews with 90 disabled people (Kleinschmidt, personal communication). Kelvin and Jarrett (1985) have argued that the concept of *identity* is the single most important factor influencing health and well-being.

There is a large literature on the psychological benefits of work and the negative effects of unemployment on mental health (see for example, Warr, 1982; 1984; 1985; Fagin and Little, 1984). From some perspectives, the aim of getting people into work is not to reduce unemployment per se but rather to realise the potential of work as treatment (Shepherd, 1989). The relationships between work and well-being are not always straightforward, however. One small study which asked mental health service users to rate 14 aspects of their job, and then related ratings to well-being scores, found that only one element (public perception of the usefulness of the job) was positively associated with well-being (Dick and Shepherd, 1994).

Arguably, meaningful activity is more important than the formal context in which it takes place.

> The need to define work, employment and leisure is more important to the funding agencies than to the person with a disability trying to lead a normal life. By making available a range of activity that encourages individual progression and assists in realising potential, much can be gained. (Coulson, 1997, p 7)

What work means to disabled people has seldom been explored from their perspective. Some people we consulted questioned whether disabled people were any different from non-disabled people, while others pointed to the

particular importance to disabled people of attaining a 'normal' status through work. It is noted that for young disabled people the status of being employed is a mark of transition to adulthood (Hirst and Baldwin, 1994). Kettle (1979) also suggests that the work role may help to compensate for feelings of loss after the onset of impairment.

> "A job takes you out of the helpless, dependent stereotype because you are actually contributing, you are a tax-payer, you are contributing to an organisation – a sense of 'I am somebody'."

A research project being carried out jointly by the Policy Studies Institute (PSI) and Disability Research Unit at the University of Leeds (DRUL) aimed "to undertake the first systemic examination of the obstacles to disabled people's full participation in society" (PSI/DRUL, 1995). This approach recognises that barriers to employment cross other societal, material or environmental barriers outside the workplace.

Employment is seldom addressed within theoretical writing on the social model of disability, however, and how far the social model can be applied in employment is open to debate.

> The paradox when you try to work to the social model is that people are judged by their physical and mental abilities – just how do you square that circle? (Lunt and Thornton, 1994)

The disabled people's movement, alongside allies in research organisations, has tried to influence the way research is done, arguing for the involvement of disabled people at all stages from the creation of ideas to the analysis and reporting of the findings. Achieving adequate funding from mainstream funding bodies has been problematic, particularly where extra resources are needed to facilitate the employment of disabled researchers (Zarb, 1997). Disabled people's organisations have led the way in research which takes as its starting point the views and experiences of disabled people. Where the research agenda has been set by disabled people themselves, assumptions about the institutionally-based objectives of policies can be challenged and research questions can be framed in terms of barriers to social participation. Experiential research can be effective in bringing about change but, as yet, there are few qualitative accounts of working as a disabled person.

> "It is more valuable to hear how it really is. The more stories you hear, the richer the research will be."

Few research studies start by asking disabled people what they want and get from work. One exploratory qualitative study involving people with learning disabilities identified the intrinsic rewards of activity and social contact in work settings but was inconclusive on attitudes to wages mostly because many participants in the study had no wages (Di Terlizzi, 1997). The role of pay in determining 'worth' has been identified as a question for future research (disabled person consulted; Corden, 1997).

There is also a research literature which reports on the effects of being in certain types of employment for particular groups of disabled people. Positive effects of being in supported employment, for example, include increased satisfaction with life (Bass and Drewett, 1997). Shepherd (1997) cites Pilling's 1988 review of the role of work in the rehabilitation of service users with continuing care needs which, however, found that the evidence of its effectiveness was weak.

Recent work by Hyde (1998) shows that many disabled workers in sheltered and supported employment feel ambivalent about their situation. On the one hand it is experienced as secure, relative to the difficulties involved in finding work in the open labour market. On the other, recent policy changes which have required sheltered workshops to become competitive have created intense pressures in terms of productivity targets. At the same time, supported employment placements often fail to deliver on their promises of integration, with disabled workers reporting stigma, reduced privileges and opportunities for overtime, and unrealistic expectations about output.

One project is developing measures of social and health outcomes for mental health service users which reflect the priorities of service users themselves rather than those traditionally adopted by mental health professionals. The project, funded by the Department of Health (DoH) as part of the programme of work on the outcomes of social care for adults (OSCA) is based at the National Schizophrenia Fellowship and being carried out in conjunction with the University of East Anglia, the Royal College of Psychiatrists and the Royal College of Nursing. These outcome measures, while not identical with the 'quality of life' concept, should provide valuable indicators of the relative importance of employment in the lives of disabled individuals as a whole.

3

Disabled people and the labour market

Researching the facts and figures

> "What is desperately needed are facts and figures: how many people are getting jobs, is it falling, is it going up in the various sectors – the numbers, how many, how long for? And also the *quality* of work that people are getting."

A string of random sample surveys commissioned by government have examined the participation of disabled people in the labour market (Martin et al, 1988; Prescott-Clarke, 1990; Sly et al, 1995; Sly, 1996). Their usefulness in showing changes over time is limited because of varying definitions of disability, differing population bases, variation in reporting methods and inconsistent understandings of economic activity or inactivity (Sly et al, 1995). A fundamental criticism is the exclusion from the economically active population in certain studies of 'discouraged workers' – those who have given up hope of ever finding a job because of labour market conditions or assumptions of structural discrimination (Hyde, 1996), or whose aspirations are limited by family or professional pressure (Rickell, 1997).

Writers in the disabled people's movement have challenged the way in which the questions have been posed in most surveys, notably the OPCS disability surveys (Abberley, 1992), which assume that impairment, rather than the social and physical environment, is the barrier to employment opportunities.

To date the Labour Force Survey (LFS), now carried out quarterly, has offered the most reliable comparative data over time, but even that has been affected by changes in survey

methods from spring 1996. The LFS asks respondents whether they have a health problem or disability, expected to last for more than 12 months, which limits the kind of paid work they can do. As do most surveys, it reports on the employment of disabled people according to their impairment, either medically or functionally defined.

According to an analysis of the LFS Winter 1995/96 (Sly, 1996):

- almost half of respondents with long-term work-limiting health problems or disabilities reported problems with their 'musculo-skeletal system' as their main problem;

- mental illness, in the form of 'depression, neuroses and phobias', was reported by 7%;

- people with long-term health problems are half as likely as those with no long-term health problems to be economically active (that is, in employment or defined as unemployed) – 40% as against 83%;

- only 15% of those with long-term mental illness are economically active;

- 28% of people with severe or specific learning difficulties are economically active;

- 57% of those with difficulty in seeing are economically active;

- those with hearing problems (64%) are most likely to be economically active.

Looking specifically at unemployment, a similar pattern emerges. Unemployment rates for disabled people were around two-and-a-half times those for non-disabled people, with the highest unemployment rates recorded for people with severe learning difficulties (38%)

and mental health problems (31%), while those with hearing difficulties had the lowest recorded unemployment rate (16%).

A completely new set of data is emerging as a result of the DDA. The DfEE, with co-funding from the ES, commissioned the Institute of Employment Studies, in conjunction with NOP Social and Political, to carry out a survey intended to provide baseline information on the employment of disabled people against which any future changes can be monitored. This survey uses the DDA definitions which are, however, currently under review. A total of 2,015 disabled people of working age were interviewed, and the report is expected in Summer 1998.

Another, already available, source of data is the Omnibus Survey carried out by the Office for National Statistics in the first three months of 1996 (Whitfield, 1997). A 'module' of questions especially for the Department of Social Security (DSS) was designed to find out the proportion of the population covered by the DDA (see Table 1). The DDA definition is distinct from those of previous studies in that it is based on 'functional' activities and includes past disability. Respondents were asked whether they currently had a long-standing illness, disability or infirmity which has affected, or was likely to affect, them for a period of time. Those who answered positively were then asked if this limited their activities in any way. People with no current long-standing condition were asked if they had ever had a long-term illness or disability which limited their activities.

The survey found marked differences in the functional problems reported by people covered by the DDA of working age, depending on whether they were in work or not, as Table 2 shows. Those with only one functional problem are most likely to be in employment; two thirds of those in work reported only one functional problem, compared with four in ten of the disabled population of working age.

Further analysis of large-scale surveys can provide powerful evidence of inequalities in employment which are not immediately apparent from the basic data. Using the OPCS disability survey data from 1985 combined with Family Expenditure Survey data, Berthoud et al (1993) found that disabled men earned less than non-disabled men – by between £1.00 and £1.50 an hour at 1985 prices – even when all the relevant factors, including occupation, are taken into account. A new investigation of the relationship between qualifications, occupation and earnings might illuminate the common claim that disabled people are 'underemployed' in jobs beneath their capacity, as well explore any hidden discrimination in paying disabled people less for equal jobs.

The limitations of surveys

While centrally commissioned surveys can explore the barriers to and in employment, opportunities to apply a social model of disability are limited as surveys are commonly tied to national definitions of disability, whether medical or 'functional'.

Table 1: Employment of men and women of working age covered by the 1995 Disability Discrimination Act compared to the general population

Characteristics	% covered by DDA	% in general population
Full-time		
Men	27	67
Women	23	38
Total	25	52
Part-time		
Men	5	7
Women	20	29
Total	13	18
Unweighted base	1,263	5,797

Source: Whitfield (1997, Table 2.3).

Survey results, despite their limitations, need to be made both more widely available and more transparent.

> "People are talking about different things, but the figures get lumped together. Figures are used inaccurately, and they don't add up. Accurate statistics are important."

There is a demand for information about who is excluded from employment – whether by age, type of impairment, access requirements, skill levels or geographical location. Most survey results give a national picture. Information about the situation of disabled people in local labour markets is increasingly necessary with the current emphasis on local projects designed to meet the needs of excluded groups, as noted by Pozner et al (1996) in their review of mental health work projects. The distribution of employment opportunities is also a rights issue: Delany (1998) points out that because of the predominance of small firms (which are exempt from the provisions of the DDA) in rural areas, people in such areas effectively have fewer rights than their peers in urban areas.

In our consultations with disabled people they identified other questions about the employment situation which surveys might answer:

- how long do disabled people stay in jobs, compared with non-disabled people?

- are disabled people less well represented in certain employment sectors (for example, the health sector)?

- how does disabled people's career progression compare?

- are disabled people to be found throughout the employing organisation – are disabled people concentrated in jobs which require particular skills, or are people with learning difficulties concentrated together?

- does 'body image' limit opportunities: for example, are disabled women fairly represented in 'front-of-house' jobs?

- are disabled people fairly represented in positions where they manage other people?

- how many people become disabled in post and leave their jobs?

Questions such as these challenge conventional ways of looking at disability and occupation and indicate the value of involving disabled people, not just in the setting of survey questions but also in determining the analysis.

New ways of working

> "These are our jobs – this is an issue we should be looking at now, before it gets any worse."

Table 2: Functional problems reported by people of working age covered by the 1995 Disability Discrimination Act

Reported functional problem	% in work	% not in work	All
Lifting and carrying	58	67	64
Mobility	17	53	39
Physical coordination	15	50	37
Learning and understanding	30	35	34
Seeing and hearing	18	23	21
Manual dexterity	16	22	20
Continence	5	13	10
Perceptions of risk	6	9	8
Unweighted base	248	1,013	1,261

Note: columns total more than 100% as people could report more than one functional problem.
Source: Whitfield (1997, Table 2.6).

The impact of the changing job market is a key concern for disabled people. The literature and the consultations identify some of the problems:

- many disabled people lack the skills required by today's labour market, largely as a result of problems in accessing education and training (Prescott-Clarke, 1990);

- the spread of new technology has led to a decrease in unskilled jobs, many of which used to be filled by disabled people (Floyd, 1995);

- employers look for the ability to work within the organisation's culture and to learn on the job (disabled participants in telephone conference);

- people are expected to be multi-skilled, and have the ability to switch between tasks in the workplace (Nodder, 1993);

- team building, leadership skills exercises *can knock the confidence of disabled people and make them feel less of a member of a team*;

- the predominance of service-based jobs, and of team-based working, places a premium on communication skills which disadvantages those with impaired speech or language (Parr et al, 1997) and Deaf people in hearing environments;

- the increase in white-collar jobs, which rely on literacy and numeracy skills, affects the employment prospects of people with learning difficulties (disabled person consulted).

The application of technology

An acutely felt problem for disabled people consulted was the rapid development of technology and the need to catch up.

> "We are being left behind in the IT field – how can we get involved?"

Despite the potential benefits of information technology (IT) for disabled people, this is an area which historically received insufficient attention from funders of employment initiatives such as the European Social Fund (Moreton, 1992).

Not all of the available training is geared to the needs of the labour market. One project,

funded by the European Social Fund, offered computer training in Surrey libraries for people who had been unemployed for six months or more, including disabled people. Of the 210 people who completed the evaluation, 96 had obtained employment following the course; over half of this employment was part time. There was no analysis by disability. Most people had enjoyed the course and several said that they had found it helpful in obtaining work, either because of the specific skills acquired, or because of a general increase in confidence. However, there were requests both for courses at a more basic level and for a course which would give people 'employment-ready' skills, suggesting that IT training needs to be carefully targeted for maximum benefit.

Another project providing IT training to disabled people surveyed the specific skills sought by employers in the area by looking at 100 job vacancies and found that employers valued work experience more than qualifications (Garforth, 1997). A mismatch between the types of software packages used by employers and those in which the project was able to offer training was also identified; this was largely because the project lacked funding to update its resources regularly.

Even in the area of technology, some of the greatest barriers to employment opportunities for disabled people are created by the attitudes of other people (Hunt and Berkowitz, 1992, cited in Moreton, 1992, p 86). A third of the disabled people interviewed by Roulstone (1998) in his study of 'enabling technology' felt that the pace of change was too much for them. Women in particular felt threatened and insecure because of inadequate training in the use of new technology. The application of technology in business can work against the employment of disabled people in other ways.

> "It leads to standardisation – human intelligence is replaced by standard processes. What we have to offer is human skills."

A small number of people in Roulstone's survey found that they came under pressure to increase output when new technology was introduced and were inhibited from taking necessary breaks. On the other hand, the same survey found that people with severe and visible impairments reported benefits from communicating via word-processing and e-mail which helped to put across their abilities and create an air of efficiency which co-workers otherwise underestimated.

Flexible working

Some ambivalence has been expressed about whether flexible employment offers more benefits or disadvantages for disabled people. Forms of flexibility such as part-time work, job-sharing, working from home (teleworking), flexible hours and annual hours, may offer disabled people a way of accommodating requirements arising from their impairment, in the same way as they offer parents and those with caring responsibilities a means of reconciling work and family life. New Ways to Work, a national organisation which promotes flexible working patterns and offers individual membership and a regular newsletter, will shortly be producing an information leaflet aimed specifically at disabled people.

Creating such flexible arrangements may be a 'reasonable adjustment' under the DDA, yet many employers would not think of this. One of our telephone discussions mentioned the case of a disabled person who wanted to work at home, and the reluctance of his employer who was concerned that this would lead to unmanageable requests for home-based working from other staff.

Teleworking, which, at face value, appears to offer many potential benefits for disabled people, has not been as quick to develop as had been anticipated. This is partly because of the costs involved for small businesses, and the lack of adequate technical systems, but also because employers are ignorant of the possibilities. Some employers are resistant to the idea, being prepared to countenance it only in cases where the employees involved are highly skilled, highly paid, and therefore in a strong bargaining position. Because of the under-representation of disabled people in professional occupations, their access to teleworking has been particularly limited. The COMBAT initiative, funded by the European Commission, has sought to extend awareness of the possibilities for teleworking both for disabled workers and for those left redundant as a result of industrial restructuring (such as miners) by the provision of three pilot

sites, one in the public and two in the private sector, offering services to local organisations (HOP 1997). The Automobile Association is currently piloting teleworking for call handling and will be evaluating this initiative, which has included the recruitment of four disabled people.

Part-time work

Research funded by the DfEE and published in October 1996 predicted that 1.5 million jobs will be created over the next ten years but half will be part time and the rest will be from self-employment. The numbers in full-time jobs are unlikely to rise (cited in New Ways to Work Annual Report 1996/97).

Disabled people are already more likely than non-disabled people to work part time. It is reasonable to suggest that the expansion of part-time work could enhance opportunities for disabled people who may prefer part-time hours for a number of household and personal reasons. These include having to devote more time to everyday living tasks such as personal care or childcare, or requiring time for treatment or therapy. Certain impairments or conditions may cause mental and physical fatigue, creating a need for part-time employment (Davoud, 1980). However, if disabled people are to benefit from part-time working, jobs and the benefits system obviously must provide adequate income to meet their needs. Combining a number of 'very part-time' opportunities to provide adequate income may be particularly problematic.

There is inconclusive evidence about disabled people's preferences for full-time or part-time work (Berthoud et al, 1993; Rowlingson and Berthoud, 1996). It is suggested that women are more likely to prefer part-time work (Thomas, 1992) and that disabled men do not perceive part-time employment as a 'real job' (Rowlingson and Berthoud, 1996). One national survey found that three quarters of disabled respondents could work a normal full-time week, while only 7% could work up to 15 hours (Prescott-Clarke, 1990). This finding is in marked contrast to actual patterns of full-time and part-time work. The analysis of data from an omnibus survey (Whitfield, 1997) found that the proportion of men working full time and covered by the DDA declined strikingly as age increased, while the proportions for men in the general population increased. Research might explore further, and whether disabled people work part time out of choice or because there is no full-time alternative, the barriers to full-time work.

Self-employment

> "... people trying to side-step the barriers by becoming self-employed, with resulting isolation, and so on, who in ideal circumstances would prefer to be employed but are making do with being self-employed, and all that entails."

Self-employment, which has grown remarkably in the last two decades, is often portrayed as an entrepreneurial opportunity. It is generally agreed that some of the growth has come from sub-contracting, home-working and franchising which are insecure and relatively poorly paid, however. Many small businesses and other forms of self-employed work are short lived and there is evidence that self-employment brings only modest financial rewards (Eardley and Corden, 1996). Self-employment involves financial risk-taking and unpredictable and fluctuating income.

Self-employment is already favoured by a sizeable minority of disabled people, who are slightly more likely than non-disabled people to be self-employed (Sly, 1996). Over two thirds are men, and a high proportion work from home and in a disability-related area (Floyd, 1995). Many report having chosen self-employment to accommodate a need for flexible working hours, or problems using transport (Thomas, 1992; Floyd, 1995). Self-employed people, whether disabled or non-disabled, tend to work longer hours. The pressures of working on one's own account can make it difficult for disabled people to work less than full hours, although a much higher proportion of self-employed than employed disabled people report that they cannot work full hours (Prescott-Clarke, 1990). Related to self-employment is the development of portfolio working, where individuals 'sell' a variety of skills either to employers or on a self-employed basis (Handy, 1994). This may be undertaken

either as a matter of choice or out of necessity, where full-time work is unavailable or impracticable.

There are a number of special schemes which are designed to promote self-employment among disabled people but a smaller number of projects which assist disabled and non-disabled people alike. Many schemes naturally teach business skills but Busby (1991) suggests that training for self-employment should include the opportunity to build or rebuild confidence, stress management and assertiveness training.

Many questions remain unanswered about disabled people's experiences of self-employment:

- who is self-employed and what types of work are being done?

- what are the factors that lead disabled people to become self-employed – is it a negative or positive choice?

- what mainstream or specialist advice and support do disabled people want to start up in and sustain self-employment?

- what is 'successful' self-employment and what are the costs?

- what happens to disabled people whose self-employment fails?

Casual and temporary jobs

The probability of having several jobs in one lifetime has increased. The flexibility required to change jobs may be more problematic for disabled people who may have to organise various support services. Working a series of temporary jobs may pose extra difficulties. If temporary work is too sporadic in nature, there is little possibility to plan wider social supports, such as personal care, transport and childcare arrangements. Adjustments made for one job are not necessarily transferable and working aids may be lost altogether if there is a gap between jobs. Income insecurity is particularly problematic for people whose disabilities impose extra costs and who are unlikely to have accumulated savings to draw upon (McLaughlin, 1994).

New forms of work

Alternatives to conventional paid work may have a particular appeal to disabled people.

Volunteering

Several sources identify a potential role for volunteering as an *alternative* to paid work providing "an opportunity for meaningful activity somewhere between paid employment and traditional voluntary work" (Kingston JCAG, 1997). For those who are not able to work, volunteering may fulfil many of the positive functions of employment:

> With the exception of a wage, it offers many of the same benefits; the chance to make decisions and shoulder responsibilities, to regain self-esteem lost through unemployment and incapacity, to develop existing skills and acquire new ones. For disabled people in particular it offers a chance to do something they themselves have independently chosen to do; for once, control of their lives has not been taken over by others. (Niyazi, 1996, p 6)

One organisation, however, commented that some local authorities need to be educated out of thinking that disabled people only need to be 'occupied' rather than wanting employment.

Although 23 million people in Britain are involved in volunteering, at present very few of them are disabled. Traditional voluntary organisations (many of which operate within a medical model of disability) tend to rely on informal recruitment practices which exclude disabled people and people from minority ethnic groups (Home Office, 1995). Organisations which have successfully recruited and retained disabled volunteers stress the importance of providing demanding roles for volunteers and of having disabled people in control of the organisation. There is also a need to create a culture of equality, with training for both staff and volunteers, and awareness of such issues as out-of-pocket expenses and concerns about benefits which can act as barriers to participation (Niyazi, 1996). A recent survey found that almost a third of organisations had lost volunteers because of fears of losing incapacity benefits; although voluntary work of less than

16 hours a week is specifically permitted as 'exempt work', it may still lead to questions about fitness for work (Home Office, 1995; CPAG, 1997/98). Organisations can help by providing advice, and by building good relationships with the local benefit office (Reilly, 1994).

The DoH has recently announced the awards under its Opportunities for Volunteering Scheme, which has a budget of approximately £140,000. Of 25 projects funded for 1998/99, nine are disability-related, and primarily concerned with the provision of information and advice.

'Third sector employment'

The growth of disabled people's organisations has brought about new opportunities for paid and unpaid work. What is sometimes known as 'third sector employment', akin to cooperative modes of organisation, differs from traditional notions of employment, with distinctive aims of empowerment for those who work within it and rejection of dominant forms of oppressive social relationships (Thornton and Lunt, 1998: forthcoming). For some disabled people, work in such organisations can be an end in itself and an alternative to conventional forms of employment, more than a source of work experience as a preliminary to 'real' work. Working within a disabled person's organisation allows an identity as a disabled person and a platform for a voice (Niyazi, 1996). The Greater Manchester Coalition of Disabled People, recognising that disabled people are best placed to provide advice to other disabled people, has a policy of recruiting only disabled people as paid staff or volunteers.

It seems that lessons might be learnt from the experience of voluntary or 'third sector' work, for example:

- what attracts disabled people?

- do disabled people's organisations make better employers?

- how transferable is good practice to mainstream employment?

As Morris (1994) argues, when user-controlled organisations employ someone, they aim to recruit people like those using the service to plan and deliver it, and this practice may by applied to other social services organisations. The difficulties that some disabled people's organisations in the review were experiencing in attracting disabled recruits – despite efforts to eliminate barriers within reach – suggest that external barriers stand in the way of both sorts of work, however.

Social firms

European funding and exchange networks have brought a resurgence of interest in the UK in alternative forms of employment, such as social employment cooperatives and social firms (Grove et al, 1997). They seem primarily to be set up *for* people with mental health problems and, to a lesser extent, people with learning difficulties. However, there is evidence that disabled people are setting up their own organisations of this nature, and that there are acknowledged benefits to such an approach to employment, although not for everyone. For some the structures available are useful, as with Abilities, a cooperative of disabled people analysing tachographs in the West Country. For others, the way that work within the organisation can be organised is the key to their usefulness, as with a self-advocacy group of people with mental health problems running a range of 'eco' projects in Nottingham. There are, however, concerns that there may be a danger of these types of work organisation becoming just an alternative 'day centre'.

The 'professionalisation' of disability

Much of the academic research has viewed being disabled in work as a negative experience and a barrier to a 'normal' quality of life. However, some experiential accounts point to the benefits of being valued in employment as a disabled person. In occupations such as nursing or other caring services, some disabled people report the personal rewards of employing their own experience of chronic illness or disability to provide better, more valued care (Sutherland, cited in Moon, 1990; O'Hare and Thompson, 1991). Changing the organisational culture to accept disability as a qualification for the job is another matter, and it may be necessary to demonstrate empirically that patients or clients do benefit. A project by the British Deaf Association, supported by JRF, found that the presence of Deaf staff in specialist services

provided by voluntary and statutory agencies increased Deaf users' confidence in them (*Findings*, Social Care Research 77, January 1996).

Increasingly, disabled people seem to be choosing occupations in which the experience of being disabled is not just an asset but a qualifying condition. People taking part in the consultations reported that disabled people were working as trainers of other disabled people or of employers, and others stressed the need for development in this area. There has perhaps been more research interest in the experience of disabled people as social policy researchers than in any other profession. Some disabled people in the performing arts report using their disability to gain work, a choice facilitated by a growing 'disability circuit' and growing public interest in disability as an issue (Taylor, 1998).

Research by Young et al, 1998, compares the issues which arose (and the ways in which they were tackled) from the employment of Deaf staff in three different workplaces, a school and two psychiatric units. In all three workplaces, the vast majority of Deaf people were employed in unqualified grades, whilst the reverse was true of hearing staff. Deaf people had been recruited for their unique skills, such as empathy and native signing ability, which were of immense benefit to children and patients in allowing them to feel at home and providing positive role models. There were tensions between the 'added value' contributed by Deaf staff and the unqualified positions they held; qualified staff felt that their professionalism was being undermined by bringing in untrained staff to do similar work. Only one workplace had been really successful in making organisational changes which allowed Deaf people to become fully integrated members of the staff team.

There is a fine line between reaping personal rewards from working as a disabled person and being exploited. Some of the disabled people we consulted were in support of policies which value 'diversity' in the workplace, while others warned of the exclusion of disabled people whose employment promotes no commercial advantages. Although the 'business case' for employing disabled people appears to have widespread support among their advocates, nothing is known about the experiences and views of disabled people working in companies which espouse such policies. Some people commented on the pressures on them to sustain the image of the more loyal, hard-working and conscientious employee which is widely promoted in government propaganda and subscribed to by some organisations of and for disabled people.

Accessing the labour market

So what are the barriers to accessing the labour market in the first place? Our consultation highlighted two barriers of particular concern to disabled people: the education system; and the benefits system.

Education

> "It all begins with education … if you don't come out with these abilities realised, you start about 500 yards back from everybody else and you spend the rest of your life catching up."

For those who are born disabled or who acquire an impairment in early childhood, experiences of education may be a significant factor affecting their readiness for work. The segregation of disabled from non-disabled people may also affect the attitudes of non-disabled people within the workplace, because of their lack of familiarity with disabled people as colleagues. People who had attended special schools felt that they had been educationally disadvantaged and had restricted aspirations as a result (Rickell, 1997). The experience of isolation and segregation may have an effect on social skills and emotional maturity. Where individuals have spent considerable periods of their childhood in hospital, basic levels of literacy and numeracy may be poor. The need for positive role models of successful employment for young people in education was cited.

For those disabled people who obtain the qualifications to enter higher education, there is often a real problem getting access to appropriate resources. Among the problems cited by individuals and in the research literature there was a lack of suitable teaching materials for disabled people, especially those with learning difficulties and dyslexia, a lack of flexibility on the part of teaching staff, and

problems in obtaining funding for postgraduate study. Issues for disabled students in further and higher education have recently been considered by the Tomlinson committee, which reported in 1996. This committee conducted a review of research both in the United Kingdom and abroad, itself commissioned research, carried out a mapping exercise to determine the extent of need and provision and consulted widely with a range of individuals and organisations.

The benefits system

Throughout the review, barriers created by the benefits system were highlighted – by those taking part in the telephone and face-to-face discussions, and in the call for ideas and experiences – and featured in much of the research (see, for example, Rickell, 1997). Concerns included:

- the difficulty of obtaining work experience through voluntary or part-time work;

- the risk of leaving benefits to take up employment which might not work out;

- the shortage of jobs which pay more than the benefit level;

- barriers to the development of supported employment;

- the role of benefits in shaping attitudes and expectations about employment for individuals, in particular the perverse effects of the 'all work' test;

- problems for those who are not judged sufficiently ill or disabled to qualify for Incapacity Benefit, but are rejected by employers because of a disability or health problem.

There is already a substantial amount of evidence from research on the disincentives or barriers built into the benefits system. The priority is to build on what is already known and test out solutions. Several sets of proposals for change have been circulated by organisations with disability income interests, ranging from adjustments which would allow people to work longer hours for more pay without losing their incapacity benefit, to a completely new 'disability income' which could be carried over into work, adjusted according to the level of earnings.

Part Two
Getting work and staying in work

4

Preparing for work

Identifying skills and strengths

Feelings of lack of confidence, together with a lack of knowledge of how to present oneself in applications and interviews, were identified by a number of disabled people and research sources (for instance Zahno and Wurr, 1996). One organisation of disabled people reported that applicants for jobs

> "... obviously didn't have that much training ... basic training, and you complete an application form, refer to the job description and things like that."

Short courses aimed at improving skills and self-confidence are not always enough to redress the effects of being 'beaten down over the years' through repeated rejection by employers. Some people mentioned a tendency for disabled people to limit themselves to jobs which they felt were well within their capabilities. Over-protective parents sometimes discourage employment, and even social activities, especially among people with learning disabilities (Cornes, 1994).

Moreton (1992) points out that not only are non-disabled people (whether as individual teachers or parents, or in society as a whole) responsible for creating poor self-image and lack of confidence among disabled people, but they also have difficulty thinking laterally about solutions because they approach problems from the perspective of a non-disabled person. This points to the importance of disabled people as trainers and facilitators, although Moreton does not draw this conclusion. He argues that counselling might be of benefit in changing the self-image of disabled people, and notes that

although a great many projects describe themselves as offering counselling, most of it is advice-giving and not of the therapeutic type. Many disabled people recognise the damaging effects of internalised oppression, but would dispute the need for 'professional' counselling input, arguing that they are more likely to gain from sharing experiences with other disabled people and mobilising around the social model of disability (Mason and Reiser, 1990).

Some disabled people are given advice which tends to limit their aspirations; for instance self-employment is often discouraged by Disabled Employment Advisors (DEAs) (Smith et al, 1991) because it is seen as inherently risky, and disabled young people wanting careers in the arts are discouraged by parents and teachers who urge them to be more 'realistic' in their aims (Arts Council of Great Britain, 1993). For children, positive role models provided by seeing disabled actors (Taylor, 1998) or Deaf teachers or health staff (Young et al, 1998) may be a valuable boost to their self-esteem, and a corrective to low expectations. Mentoring has been identified as one way in which disabled people with successful employment histories can pass on skills and confidence (Redfern, personal communication). However, there are currently too few disabled people at senior levels for this to be widely available on an informal level, and paid services are beyond the reach of most disabled people.

Disability can, of course, be a positive attribute in seeking work, either because the work involves knowledge and experience of disability, or simply because of the problem-solving skills and organisational abilities which disabled people develop when dealing with

22

issues in their own lives. It is argued that disabled nurses could contribute valuable inside knowledge on patient care (Moon, 1990) and that disabled people working in caring professions bring valuable knowledge of disability and an ability to empathise (French, 1995).

However, some of the literature, as well as personal experiences which were reported to us, suggests that disabled people working in 'caring' professions such as nursing, medicine or physiotherapy had met with particularly unhelpful reactions from their employers. French (1988) notes that despite the emphasis on the importance of 'empathy' in the careers literature of caring professions, none of them actively encourages disabled people to apply. Her own research used several methods, including making enquiries about career prospects for fictitious applicants, a survey of attitudes amongst 35 qualified physiotherapists, and interviews with 25 disabled people working

in health and caring professions (of whom all but two were disabled prior to training). Among those in the postal survey, attitudes towards disabled people were more favourable among younger age groups and towards people with visual impairment (a group already well established in the profession).

A contrast to these negative views is presented by a project in the London Borough of Wandsworth which has sought to make positive use of the experiences of people with mental health problems by employing them in mental health teams and by making personal experience as a user of mental health services an essential requirement of the posts (Perkins et al, 1997). Those recruited were given additional support (both during the application process and once in employment) from a support worker who received a nominal payment in exchange for providing practical assistance in getting to work and resolving problems which arose.

Learning from Experience Trust

The Learning from Experience Trust has produced a pack *Make your experience count* which encourages people to identify their achievements, personal qualities and transferable skills, and provides examples of how to present these in CVs and application forms, as part of a project 'Recognising Ability' (Cornell, 1997a; 1997b). The project worker has personal experience of disability and the pack was developed in conjunction with two consultation panels of disabled people, and piloted by disabled people, employers and those involved in recruitment. Feedback from all these groups was very positive; it was found that the pack was of most benefit when used in a group setting, although individuals also found it helpful (Cornell, 1997c). There is a perceived need for another version of the pack geared specifically to the needs of people with mental health problems.

Royal National Institute for the Blind Vocational College

The RNIB Vocational College (in Loughborough), with funding from DfEE, has produced a disk-based resource pack aimed at assisting individuals to maximise their self-presentation skills in order to improve their chances of obtaining and retaining employment. This was piloted in selected TEC areas and launched nationwide in 1997.

First Step Trust

The First Step Trust in Greenwich, with funding from Comic Relief, provides services for people with mental health problems to address lack of self-confidence, social isolation and office skills, as well as advocacy and rights work.

Training

Considerable scepticism about the types of training available was expressed by some of those responding to the consultation, and many shortcomings are evident from the research literature. Training is often felt to be shaped more by stereotypes about disabled people than by the changing requirements of the labour market:

> Training geared to the social model of disability would start from the premise of enabling Disabled people to plan their own preferred, individual employment strategies. Existing training funnels them down pre-determined, narrow avenues of 'dead-end' segregated provision, specialising in out-of-date and unmarketable types of employment. (Laurie and Higgins, undated, p 15)

Concern was also voiced that in some cases, new stereotypes were simply replacing old ones; the dominance of computer training for disabled people was cited as an example of this.

> "Training, forever training! How real are the jobs?"

In areas with high unemployment, such as inner London boroughs, employment was not felt to be a likely outcome of any training course. TECs were felt to have a considerable wealth of both resources and contacts which were not always being deployed for the benefit of disabled people. TEC boards have a contractual obligation to ensure equality of opportunity, and are obliged to make clear in their corporate and business plans how they plan to meet the requirements of people in their local area, including those with 'special needs' such as disability, language needs and people with literacy or numeracy problems. Independent research has been generally critical of the effectiveness of state provided training schemes, both mainstream and specialist. Criticisms drawn from users' experience include undervaluing of users' employment potential and lack of responsiveness to user preferences (Hyde, 1996).

Published outcome data on the Employment Service Training for Work programme show a clear gap between outcomes for disabled and mainstream trainees. Concern has been expressed about negative effects for disabled people of moves to gear funding towards job outcomes and away from qualification outcomes, which risks altering Training for Work from a training programme to a job placement scheme (Meager, 1995). Major variations between TEC areas in the proportions of trainees in disadvantaged groups do not reflect underlying population differences and imply either considerable imbalances in provision or widely differing endorsement procedures; it appears that many disabled people are now either classed as 'mainstream ' trainees or are not entering the Training for Work programme at all (Meager, 1995). Rolfe et al (1996) caution that people with special needs may miss out in the move towards integrated provision in the face of increased selectivity by providers and the lack of resources for special equipment and expertise. In this context, it will be important that progress towards equality targets which were imposed on TECs by the incoming government is carefully monitored. Guidance to training providers to improve access for disabled trainees is essential (see, for example, Parkinson, 1996).

Recommendations from one recent conference on disability and employment included:

- a focus on ordinary disabled people in ordinary jobs, not high achievers at the limits of what is possible;

- offering effective support to disabled people who are taking risks with their lives and their employment prospects;

- measuring success by whether employers have competent employees and a fair return on their investment, and disabled people have real jobs and increased incomes;

- funding to be tied to job outcomes, not NVQs achieved. (Parkinson and Freeney, 1997)

Research into the labour market experiences of 60 visually impaired people carried out for the RNIB (Tillsley, 1997) found that those with the highest educational qualifications were most successful in obtaining employment, leading to questions about the wisdom of an emphasis on vocational training for disabled people.

In respect of the New Deal, details of which were announced by the government in August 1997, the issue of whether the jobs created would be real or supernumerary was raised. Concern was also expressed that the programmes need to allow sufficient time for an individual to achieve 'work-readiness', for instance by making allowance for time needed to adjust both to the routines of being in work, and to procedures within the workplace.

Specialised training and work experience schemes

Certain industries and sectors have developed schemes which are aimed at increasing the employment of people within their particular industry, some of which are focused on specific impairments. For instance, Cultural Partnerships, one organisation which contacted us, is involved in training under-represented groups in arts production, including live performance, radio and video. One recent project was a 13-week course in radio production for blind people.

Several initiatives specialise in support or work experience for higher education students and graduates. Cardiff University Students' Union has recently set up a support group for disabled students, which enables students to share experiences and exchange information, for instance on employers with a positive attitude towards disabled people. A consortium of six universities has set up a web site for disabled students, based at Lancaster University (http://cando.lancs.ac.uk/). An organisation called Workable has developed a number of schemes which provide work experience, aimed at assisting disabled graduates to enter employment in specific areas; for instance insurance, media and the legal profession.

Work experience through volunteering

In addition to providing an alternative to paid work, volunteering may act as a pathway into employment (MacFarlane, 1997). However, although this potential is frequently emphasised by organisations which employ volunteers, we know little about how many people do go on to paid employment, nor about how positively employers regard experience gained as a volunteer. Although many disabled people gain experience in their own organisations, these may not have the resources to formalise a structured work experience programme.

In Tendring in Essex a series of projects have been set up for, and run by, disabled people with this purpose as one of their primary objectives (Reilly, 1994). This was based on the finding that disabled people surveyed in the area doubted their ability to hold down a job, in terms of punctuality, attendance and so on, even if it were offered. The Hull-based DUET offers advice, support and training for unemployed disabled people. It has almost 100 volunteers of whom only 12 do not consider themselves to be disabled. Access to voluntary work is not necessarily straightforward, however, and people with learning difficulties report prejudice when trying to obtain work experience by volunteering (disabled person consulted).

Abilities

Abilities is a training organisation run by disabled people for disabled people, with funding from Comic Relief, to help obtain employment and develop self-employment opportunities. It provides training in office management and administrative skills, and works with training agencies and employers to help find suitable paid employment.

5

Finding and applying for jobs

Transitions into work

One of the areas which was identified as a priority for research was the ways in which disabled people 'fall out of the system'. This may be particularly likely to happen at times of transition, for instance from school to work or training, or from training or higher education into work. Research into the transition from school to adult working life for people with learning difficulties has recently begun at the Welsh Centre for Learning Difficulties Applied Research Unit. Cheshire County Council Supported Employment have run a project concerned with enabling young people to make a smooth transition from education to employment.

Services for accessing work

Special versus mainstream

Some organisations reported that their involvement with both disabled and non-disabled clients was the key to their success. Essex Returners' Unit had originally targeted mature men and women returning to the labour market, but has since expanded to meet the needs of disabled returners. Next Step offers joint training for self-employment and paid employment to both disabled and non-disabled people; once appropriate equipment has been organised, disability is not an issue. Another initiative, Training into Employment, trains people who have been long-term unemployed to be the support workers of people with learning disabilities.

In contrast, there was criticism of some schemes among the disabled people consulted. In describing her personal experience, one person described a scheme run by a charity and several large companies as "poor quality", and "not proper management training"; another participant also cited "stupid schemes" as part of the barriers facing disabled people.

One organisation was asked to pilot a wage subsidy for disabled people, funded by the EU and administered by the local TEC. This provided £85 per week, which could be used to integrate the disabled person in the workplace, offer training, pay for equipment or simply underwrite wage costs or the costs of starting in self-employment. This was successful in enabling several disabled people to set up small businesses, although the conditions applicable to employers effectively excluded all but a minority from taking part. Another organisation, funded by three Scottish local authorities and with subsidies from both the DfEE and the European Social Fund, was aimed at increasing the employment rate of disadvantaged groups in the area, by offering wage subsidies of between 40 and 60% to employers. It was successful in creating around 3,000 additional jobs, most of which lasted over three years, and from which two-thirds of leavers went into alternative employment, at a unit cost of about £3,500. However, most of the jobs created were in work with fairly low skill levels (possibly reflecting a ceiling on the amount of subsidy available) and only 5% of those taking part were disabled, despite disabled people being identified as a target group. Recommendations from the evaluation of this scheme included paying a differential rate of subsidy for disabled and non-disabled people, and the building of closer links between employers and sources of assistance for equipment and advice about disability issues.

Agencies

The predominance of agency work in certain sectors can be a barrier to employment. Disabled people are often not well served by mainstream employment agencies, although some innovative large employers who use temporary agencies may require them to supply a quota of disabled staff. Even where agencies are willing to find work for disabled people, delays in obtaining equipment can mean that job opportunities are lost.

> "The people they are getting you a job with want you there tomorrow morning, not in six months' time."

Questions identified for further research include:

- what are the attitudes of agencies towards disabled people?

- to what extent are agencies involved in supplying disabled workers?

- what are their experiences of the barriers in placing disabled people in work?

Finding one job is difficult enough for disabled people, given the practical obstacles and the prevalence of discriminatory attitudes. Securing casual or temporary jobs may require outside help. The UK, as elsewhere, has seen an expansion of specialist placement agencies for disabled people and other groups thought 'hard-to-place' in the labour market. Specialist agencies can offer tailor-made support and links both to employers and to state-supported provision to facilitate access to work. Some temporary work agencies are themselves the employers, thus relieving enterprises of the risks of taking on disabled workers. There may be advantages to disabled people in this new type of opportunity to try out and make a mark in employment.

Access to and satisfaction with existing services

The quality of help provided by an adviser was cited as a crucial factor in helping an individual through 'the system', but this is often poor. Careers services are sometimes not well informed about specific impairments (especially visual impairment). Several individuals also provided us with accounts of their negative experiences of PACTs and DEAs who were considered particularly unhelpful in cases where the effects of a disability were not obvious. Improved training for DEAs, especially in the use of access software, was recommended by one organisation for blind people. A survey of members of the National Federation of the Blind revealed widespread dissatisfaction with services including PACT, DEAs and AtW. ABAPSTAS (Association of Blind and Partially Sighted Teachers and Students) has also produced proposals for change entitled 'Making Access to Work work'.

Brook Street/Friends for the Young Deaf

A commercial recruitment agency, Brook Street, and a charity for young deaf people, Friends for the Young Deaf (FYD), have worked in partnership for some years. Brook Street offers work experience and assessment to young deaf graduates leaving the FYD leadership training programme; Brook Street then places appropriate candidates into jobs, charging the usual commercial fee (Scott-Parker, 1998).

Blind in Business

Blind in Business is an organisation set up by three blind professionals. It was established to raise awareness of the role of computer technology in opening up education and employment opportunities for visually impaired people. It recently launched a Job Covenant Scheme which asks employers to covenant a job for a visually impaired person. By targeting employers who require well-qualified young people, the aim is to secure quality jobs with prospects for advancement.

Applying for work

Several people made the point that application forms posed problems for disabled people who were not able to write, and that even where applications in other forms were accepted, this sometimes created an unwelcome 'visibility' for the disabled applicant. The use of certain skills is also often used as a 'proxy' measure for employability even where these skills are not actually required. Driving was cited as an example of this, as was the ability to write. Such practices are discriminatory and are open to challenge using the DDA in firms with 20 or more employees, but the extent of protection in 'grey areas' remains to be tested. Examining the scope for continuing discrimination which exists despite the legislation was identified as a research priority.

Disabled people may need active encouragement to apply for jobs. Events such as 'job fairs' aimed specifically at disabled people, rather than all job seekers, were suggested as one way of doing this. Twenty-five companies jointly funded an initiative to make careers fairs accessible to disabled students so that they could participate in the mainstream recruitment process. Responding to employers' frustrations with such events provided by the education system, and their difficulties in recruiting disabled graduates, the companies funded and arranged wheelchair access, interpreters for Deaf people and large print brochures among other supports (Scott-Parker, 1998).

How employers recruit

Most studies of how disabled people access jobs concentrate on employers' recruitment practices, reflecting national policy concerns to encourage 'good practice'. There has been considerable investment by government in monitoring the effects on practice of codes of practice and voluntary initiatives such as the Disability Symbol and employers' networks (Morrell, 1990; Honey et al, 1993; Maginn and Meager, 1995; Dench et al, 1996). Codes of conduct tend to assume a standardised approach to job advertising, short-listing and interview. Among employers who monitor equalities issues, it has been found that only gender, race and disability issues (those covered by legislation) are monitored to a significant degree. This is usually a function of personnel staff rather than line managers and, as such, is usually concentrated on the recruitment stage (Industrial Society, 1995). A number of organisations have produced 'good practice' guides for employers wishing to employ more disabled people. The proliferation of guides relating to specific impairments may, however, be confusing and counterproductive.

One survey of employers in North London (Wills et al, undated) found a considerable mismatch between the ways in which employers sought employees and the ways in which disabled people were looking for work. Almost 80% of disabled people were using job centres, as compared to under a quarter of employers. Half of the employers were using a recruitment agency, but none of the disabled people did so, and although 12% of disabled people had used a specialist recruitment agency, none of the employers in the survey had used this agency. A survey of 700 PACT clients (Beinart et al, 1996), found that only a third of those who had entered employment since their initial assessment had learnt of the vacancy from a DEA or Jobcentre source. The majority had relied on other sources such as press advertisements, direct approaches to employers and information from friends and acquaintances.

Visually impaired people may be particularly reliant on 'word of mouth' information because of the lack of materials on tape or in Braille (Jamison, 1995); it was also suggested by one organisation for visually impaired people that their members have fewer informal contacts because of lack of access to voluntary work, integrated leisure and sports activities. A survey on the employment training and service needs of visually impaired people carried out on behalf of the London Association for the Blind (OUTSET, 1990) found that the primary need was for information, including, but not limited to, taped and Braille information. Industries which traditionally rely on personal contacts as a source of new recruits also tend to exclude disabled people as a whole (Arts Council of Great Britain, 1993).

Discrimination

Employers have been found to be more likely to turn down a disabled applicant for a job even when their qualifications are identical to those of a non-disabled person (Graham et al, 1990; Ravaud et al, 1992). People with hidden disabilities face a dilemma about disclosure when applying for jobs; not revealing the disability may improve the chances of obtaining employment, but could lead to problems later. Over two thirds of people completing a Mind questionnaire agreed that they had been put off from applying for a job because they thought they would be unfairly treated due to their psychiatric history (Read and Baker, 1996). People with particularly stigmatised conditions such as HIV, mental health problems and epilepsy may have acute anxieties about revealing their status. Pre-employment screening for health problems is not prevented by the DDA and people who cannot demonstrate that they are protected by the Act may have their employment contract terminated if they do not declare their condition. Here again is an example of potential discrimination despite the legislation. Research in progress is looking at the implications of pre-employment screening for people with epilepsy (Delany, personal communication).

One area which was raised as requiring further research was the attitudes of employers and their reasons for not employing more disabled people. It is often argued that concerns about the costs of employing a disabled person underlie employer's reluctance to hire. However, the experiences of disabled people's organisations suggest that more fundamental barriers than employers' attitudes have to be overcome. A large number of issues for further research were identified:

- the problems caused for people without access to the legal process, for example because of lack of money;

- what discrimination is continuing, despite the DDA? is it within the law or not? is it taking new and more subtle forms?;

- how can people be educated out of discrimination?;

- the complexity of experience, including issues of age, sexual orientation, ethnicity, impairment, occupation and family structure;

- the need for an understanding of how barriers to employment impact on people with different impairments; balanced by

- a focus on the barriers, and the common experience of discrimination.

6

Being at work

There is considerably less research and development activity concerned with the needs of disabled people in work than with the process of preparing for and entering employment. This is partly because these needs are not always identified. It may also be related to the measures of success which are applied to many employment initiatives, which tend to discourage long-term involvement with individuals. Some organisations, however, do see the provision of ongoing support for the disabled employee as falling within their remit. At least some responsibility for providing ongoing support also rests with employers, although they may encounter problems over alerting employees of their need for assistance.

However, many employers are unaware of the sources of support (whether financial or advisory) which are available to them if they take on a disabled worker. One survey found that DEAs also lacked knowledge about particular types of employment (Arts Council of Great Britain, 1993). The types of support which are appropriate will vary from individual to individual, and may consist of equipment, adjustments to work practices, and training for either the disabled person or their colleagues. Issues mentioned by disabled people included transport and the recognition of needs relating to work hours or flexibility (Smith et al, 1991; Wills et al, undated).

Support in the workplace

Equipment and services

The question of who is responsible in practice for securing necessary equipment under the ES

Access to Work (AtW) programme was raised several times during the consultation process. One participant in a telephone conference made the point that disabled people are usually left to resolve this themselves:

> "... you wouldn't expect that of any other employee, you wouldn't say, 'Oh, you've come, right, now where are you going to get your desk from?'"

The same point is made in one good practice guide for employers:

> ... this is not 'special provision'. Equipment and adaptations required to enable disabled people to do their job most effectively should be looked upon in the same ways as machines or other facilities which increase the efficiency of other employees, eg, word processors, childcare, etc. (DRT 1994, p 24)

DfEE has published case studies of 40 employers' practice in integrating a disabled employee which demonstrate the benefits of both individual and general adjustements (Watson et al, 1998)..

Delays in securing equipment under ATW were cited as a major problem for disabled people starting work, and one which could place the success of a job at risk. Research into the first year of operation of AtW (Beinart et al, 1996) found that staffing pressures and the requirement to obtain value for money when procuring adaptations could cause delay; a follow-up study is due to report. The experience of disabled people using this scheme was mentioned as an area in which qualitative research was required.

An evaluation (ES, 1990) of the six schemes available to disabled people prior to the introduction of ATW, found that those with certain impairments (visual impairment, diseases of the central nervous system and spinal injury) were more likely to have received help. This may partly be a reflection of the available technology, but may also indicate a tendency to concentrate on those people who can be most 'easily' helped. Around half of those who benefited from one of the schemes had been disabled since childhood, and most had been working either part time or full time immediately prior to using the scheme. Use of the special schemes was markedly less in part-time employment. It was also occupationally segregated, with a heavy concentration on non-manual jobs. A similar picture emerges from an evaluation of ATW (Beinart et al, 1996). This also seems to favour full-time work and people in clerical and professional jobs, with an over-representation of people with long-term impairments and those who are visually impaired.

Support from others

The presence of a supportive individual, whether a line manager or colleague, within the organisation is mentioned as important by a number of sources (Reynolds et al, 1997). However, some disabled people experience negative and unhelpful attitudes from colleagues. For instance, in one study people who had been provided with equipment reported feelings of resentment from colleagues (Roulstone, 1998).

Support from another person is mentioned as the primary employment need of many people with learning disabilities. For instance, MENCAP mentioned the importance of 'learning the ropes' at work. A study of people with learning difficulties who obtained work experience or training via day centres found, however, that:

> Staff support often ended or was markedly reduced soon after an introduction to the placement.... Many participants had the experience of integrated work settings, but did not have the technical assistance to improve their work performance. (Di Terlizzi, 1997, p 508)

Large firms are most likely to be aware of disability issues and to have undertaken measures such as disability equality training. Small firms have fewer resources and those employing fewer than 20 people are also currently exempt from the provisions of the DDA. However, some people responding to our consultation commented that small firms offered more support and training on an individual level, and could thus provide a better working environment for disabled people. Support for employers may also be required and they have been found to value the role of placement agency staff (Bass and Drewett, 1997; Corden and Thornton, 1997; CRG (private Consultancy Company) Research Consultancy Training, 1996).

In some organisations, voluntary work has been designed to meet the needs of people with fluctuating conditions, by accommodating short or longer periods of absence. Niyazi (1996) provides a number of practical examples of how to provide this sort of flexibility, including having 'stand-by' rotas to cover last-minute absence, keeping in touch with volunteers who are absent for long periods, and developing efficient ways of communicating changes at short notice. These suggestions could equally well be taken up by other employers, although there would obviously be greater cost implications.

Lack of support for disabled people in the workplace may lead to impossible burdens. Individuals who took part in the consultation exercise mentioned issues such as people having to take work home with them to catch up because there was insufficient time in the working day. One invidious practice within the workplace can be the 'ghettoisation' of disabled workers. In other words, disabled people are expected to work alongside or socialise primarily with other disabled people, or to provide support for them. There is also a tendency to expect the disabled employee to be an unpaid expert on all issues concerned with disability, even where this has nothing to do with their work (Reynolds et al, 1997; Arts Council of Great Britain, 1993).

Young et al (1998) found that social relationships both within and outside the workplace were important in improving work between Deaf and hearing staff. This was to some extent dependent on the commitment to signing, for instance whether there was a policy that hearing people should continue to sign in 'off-duty' times such as coffee breaks. A study carried out in the US (Foster, 1986, cited in Kyle et al, 1989) found that deaf graduates were often lonely at work because of barriers to socialising.

Personal assistance

Personal assistance for daily living and support at work may have to be financed by disabled people who need it. Charges increasingly levied by local authorities and the policy of the Independent Living Fund (which considers income above Income Support level to be available for care costs) may be disincentives. Preliminary findings from a Disablement Income Group study, supported by JRF, which interviewed 50 disabled people, highlight the satisfaction for people where support systems enable them to control their personal assistance in flexible arrangements compatible with their work patterns. They also highlight the additional physical and mental demands presented by the need to manage those arrangements on top of full-time work.

Barriers specific to impairment

Our consultations, which drew on representations from impairment-focused membership and lobby organisations, as well as from disabled people themselves, tended to emphasise the potential barriers in work facing people with specific impairments. These included visual impairment, learning disabilities, deafness, epilepsy, as well as conditions such as multiple sclerosis, cystic fibrosis, sickle cell disease, HIV and AIDS. At the same time, it was pointed out that the emphasis on recognised disabilities, or even on chronic illnesses (although these were not so well recognised within the workplace), tended to leave out of the picture not only people with multiple impairments, but also people with conditions such as back pain which do not fit into recognised categories. 'New' impairments such as ME, repetitiven strain injury and HIV were identified as particularly invisible.

There were many calls to extend the provision of information to employers and co-workers

about these impairments and chronic conditions. As noted elsewhere, many impairment-related organisations produce educational material to help employers understand the impairment and its effects. Some organisations are keen to ensure that their members' interest are adequately covered in employers' policies. However, the effectiveness of promotional material about specific impairments is rarely assessed.

People with visual impairments or learning difficulties are perceived by employers as the most difficult to employ (Dench et al, 1996). People with mental health problems also face particularly high levels of prejudice. A survey of 120 limited companies for the Royal College of Psychiatrists (Manning and White, 1995) found that 30% would 'never' or only 'occasionally' employ someone who had experienced mental health problems. Kettle (1979) found high levels of prejudice against those with epilepsy, but a survey of 200 national employers (Cooper, 1992) found good levels of understanding. Employers were only reluctant to employ people with epilepsy in potentially hazardous jobs, although such attitudes and policies may not be communicated sufficiently clearly to employees or applied at a local level.

Research by impairment-specific groups has found that the degree of impairment is a significant predictor of whether an individual will be in employment. A survey carried out for RNIB (Tillsley, 1997) found that half of those who were partially sighted were employed as against only one in six blind people. Another survey of members of the British Epilepsy Association (1,709 responses) (Collings and Chappell, 1994) found that people who were free from seizures were most likely to be in employment and also reported higher levels of satisfaction in relationships with colleagues and managers.

Employers are often sceptical about back pain as a cause of genuine incapacity for work, regarding it as a common excuse for absence (Moffett et al, 1995). Straughair (1992), researching the experiences of young people with arthritis, found that barriers to employment had included both inaccessible workplaces and low expectations on the part of ES advisers. One young woman was 'warned' that a vacancy required five 0 levels when in fact she had a degree. Arthritis was also seen to create problems in the workplace because of its status as an 'invisible' impairment.

For Deaf people, occupational profile is strongly related to the onset of impairment. Those who have been deaf since early childhood are most likely to have attended special schools and to use British Sign Language as a first or only language, and least likely to hold recognised qualifications. In contrast, those who acquire hearing loss in later life have similar qualifications and jobs to the population at large. For this latter group, the main problems are that of under-employment or curtailment of career prospects (Kyle et al, 1989). For the former, in addition to their lack of qualifications and sometimes low levels of literacy, stereotypes about their suitability for certain jobs (De Caro et al, 1982) and the unsuitability of many vocational assessment tools based on written language concepts (Kyle et al, 1989) may create barriers to appropriate employment.

Progress and promotion

The existence of a 'glass ceiling' for disabled people was mentioned a number of times during the course of the review.

> "You know, people are happy to have disabled people in their office, in their workplace, but when it comes to being managed by a disabled person ... some extra barriers come in."

Many disabled people are working in posts for which they are over qualified, and have problems getting promoted (Reynolds et al, 1997). Some disabled people report stereotyping by employers, who feel that people with physical impairments are not dynamic and lack an aura of efficiency and drive (Roulstone, 1998). These issues may be particularly acute in sectors where appearance is deemed important, or where travel is an essential feature of the work (Arts Council of Great Britain, 1993). There may be constraints, such as the cost of adapting housing, the availability of service provision or the need to remain close to existing networks, which prevent disabled people from

being geographically mobile in the way which employers may expect as part of the career progression. The issue of loyalty and feelings of guilt towards employers who have gone to a lot of trouble to make accommodations or adaptations was also mentioned as a factor which made it difficult for some disabled people to change jobs.

Deaf people often experience problems progressing in education as well as employment. This is partly because of the lack of sign language interpreters. Quality of interpretation is also a problem; skilled interpreters will, for instance, give indications of the 'atmosphere' of a meeting; without this, Deaf people in senior positions may come across as inarticulate. Misunderstandings may also be caused by incidents such as a Deaf person slamming a door (spokesperson for British Deaf Association).

Research in progress is exploring the under-representation of disabled people and people from minority ethnic groups in senior management and chief executive roles in the voluntary sector (ACENVO, personal communication).

An alternative research approach is to look at how disabled people achieve success in their chosen careers. This is the subject of PhD research currently being carried out at Loughborough University. In-depth interviews with disabled people will look at five main areas; personality, family and social background, education, training and work experience, and the nature of the impairment.

Issues for further research include:

- what would sustain people once they have found jobs?

- what are the costs and benefits of various types of support?

- what is the appropriate input to employers and from employers?

- looking at those disabled people who have had long and successful careers, are there lessons which can be applied across the board?

7 Becoming disabled in work

Becoming disabled while in work was less of an issue for the people consulted than getting into work in the first place – and staying there – when already disabled. This reflects not only the experience of the people who responded and the interests of the majority of impairment-specific disability organisations, but also the long-standing emphasis on access to work in national policy and services for disabled people.

The fact that the majority of disabled people became disabled when in work is not often acknowledged by disability organisations, whose campaign focus has been on overcoming barriers to entry to employment and reducing discrimination against disabled people who find work. Some pressure groups are ambivalent about backing support measures for workers who become disabled in work, in case attention is diverted from the barriers facing disabled people who have never worked. A notable exception is the work of organisations of and for visually impaired people, such as the National Federation of the Blind, the Wales Council for the Blind and RNIB, which have highlighted the barriers facing people who become visually impaired when in work, through campaigns, research and development projects (Winyard, 1996; Paschkes-Bell et al, 1996; Paschkes-Bell, 1997).

A new policy emphasis on keeping in work people who become disabled is emerging, however. This has been prompted by the DDA and by the Labour government's Welfare to Work programme for disabled people which aims to explore ways of reducing the rate at which people leave work and become dependent on incapacity benefits. The increase of interest is reflected by the DfEE's decision to

co-sponsor a current international study of job retention strategies for disabled people, coordinated by the Social Policy Research Unit at the University of York under the auspices of the International Labour Organisation (Thornton, 1998).

How big is the problem?

There is no readily available information about the number of people who become disabled in work and the proportion who consequently leave their employment. Professional bodies rarely monitor the position. Employing organisations tend to frame the problem of absence in terms of lost working days and effects on productivity (James et al, 1997; Cunningham and James, 1998: forthcoming). A project to promote employment of disabled people in six local authorities found that information on people leaving through ill health was not held in a way which facilitated monitoring (Erne, 1991). It is striking that analyses in government-commissioned studies, which are intended to inform the development of services to support employment of disabled people, do not differentiate between people who have become disabled in work and those who are already disabled (see Beinart, 1997, and Beinart et al, 1996).

One obstacle to achieving useful facts and figures is the standard way of defining disability. Some of those affected may not be included in the definitions of disability used in national surveys, including the DDA definition, if their condition is not predicted to last for at least 12 months or if it does not adversely affect 'normal day-to-day activities'. The 'new' occupational diseases, such as repetitive strain injury or occupational stress, and conditions such as back pain, are not usual survey categories, although it is thought that in future they are more likely to be recognised by employers as disabling conditions as a consequence of the DDA (James et al, 1997). The Health and Safety Executive is sponsoring a three-year study into 'occupational stress', involving a survey of 17,000 people, with the aims of reaching an accurate working definition of the term, considering the causes of stress at work, determining its extent and severity and assessing its effects on people's health.

There are, however, dangers in dividing the population into those who 'become disabled' and those who are 'already disabled'. People who are disabled before they take up work can be just as likely to be affected by conditions such as stress or RSI once in work. Moreover, disadvantage caused by disability can be compounded by the effects of ageing (Zarb and Oliver, 1993).

The experience of becoming disabled in work

There is little research which explores the experience of becoming disabled in work, although some studies have looked at experiences within particular professions. O'Hare and Thompson (1991) surveyed 23 physiotherapists, all of whom had become disabled after completing their training. Over half felt that their competence was unaffected, but over two-thirds said that their job prospects had been negatively affected. Nine respondents reported that they were *better* at the job because of increased levels of empathy with patients, a view also found by French (1988) in her study of physiotherapists who were disabled when they entered the profession. A small survey of 12 nurse members of the Association of Disabled Professionals (Moon, 1990) found that eight had to stop working and none was

working in the same job as before becoming disabled.

Becoming disabled may lead to redeployment to a post with less status. Alternatively it may lead to more subtle changes in the attitudes and behaviour of colleagues and managers which, nonetheless, have the effect of excluding the disabled person, a situation which Reynolds et al (1997) describe as 'sliding to the edges'. People who become disabled in work may need advocates in the workplace or support for self-advocacy.

Pressure to leave employment

Those disabled people who commented on the issue were concerned about the pressure on people who become disabled to leave their jobs. A study in Devon in the early 1990s found that of those respondents who were in employment at the time they acquired their disability, 104 (61%) left for health reasons and, of those, over half claimed they were dismissed or pressured into leaving by their employer (Hyde and Howes, 1993). The widespread practice of using early retirement on health grounds to remove from the workforce people who are still capable of work can diminish the status of those who genuinely have to retire because they are ill or disabled. Employers' over-riding desire to reduce costs was thought to determine the route out of employment, regardless of whether the employee was sick or not. One disabled person told us that she opted to resign rather than retire on health grounds, so that the money saved by the employer could be used to support the continuation of work to which she had a professional commitment.

The question was raised of how to make people aware of their rights when they become disabled in employment, emphasising the potential role of trades unions, medical professionals and social workers. General practitioners are to be targeted in an initiative led by the EFD.

Multiple Sclerosis Society: Colchester

The Colchester Branch of the Multiple Sclerosis Society has been awarded a grant of £188,000 to equip people with multiple sclerosis with the 'skills, attitudes and knowledge' which will enable them to stay in their present jobs. A series of courses for individuals and seminars for employers are being run.

In our consultations disabled people remarked on how employers' good intentions could be obstructed by health and safety requirements. Several writers have also commented on the problems that the 1974 Health and Safety at Work Act is likely to cause employers seeking to retain disabled employees, as well as the possibility that employers will use the Act as justification for discriminating against them. The pressures on employers from their employment liability insurers have also been commented on, as has the civil damages procedure which inhibits people who have been injured at work from returning to their employment when seeking to sue their employer (Pickvance, 1997). The obstructive effects of the health and safety legislation and the consequences for disabled people caught up in the system require detailed research.

Questions identified for research include:

- how far do people leave work for financial reasons, for health reasons, or to meet employer interests – and how much control does the person have over the decision?

- what is the role of the medical profession in opposing or supporting employer pressure to retire early on health grounds?

Supporting the retention of employees who become disabled

A considerable amount of research effort has been devoted to discovering whether employers have a formal policy on the employment of disabled people. Results vary depending on the methods used. Some much-cited surveys which have found that as many as 87% of companies have a written policy are misleading, because of the very low response rate and the bias towards very large employers (for example, EOR, 1997). The more reliable Multi-Purpose Survey of Employers in the spring and summer of 1996 covered 1,100 establishments and found that 45% of companies covered by the DDA had a formal policy on the employment of disabled people. However, it is important to distinguish between the inclusion of disabled people in general equal opportunities policies and policies which specifically address disabled people's employment. A random survey commissioned by government found that only 17% of establishments had such a specific policy,

compared with 48% with general policies covering disabled people among others (Dench et al, 1996).

Some research commissioned by the DfEE has looked at employers' *retention* policies, as part of their overall policies for employment of disabled people (Morrell, 1990; Honey et al, 1993; Dench et al, 1996). As with many surveys of equal opportunities policies, this research is restricted to monitoring employers' stated policies and has not examined in any depth how they are put into practice or their real effects in enabling people who become disabled to keep their jobs. The types of methods used – such as telephone interviews and self-completion questionnaires – limit their usefulness. In one centrally commissioned telephone survey of a random sample of employers virtually every respondent reported that they would be prepared to take positive steps to retain an existing employee who becomes disabled (Dench et al, 1996).

The experiences of the people who become disabled have not been explored in these studies. Other surveys have asked disabled people retrospectively about action employers did or did not take. A 1993 sample survey of recipients of the Invalidity (now Incapacity) Benefit found 27% were in employment immediately prior to their claim. Of these, three-quarters said that their employers had provided no assistance to help them carry on working (Erens and Ghate, 1993). James et al (1997) reviewed survey evidence of employers' policies and arrangements to prevent ill health and assist the return to work of those who are absent through illness. They found that the only survey to explore in any depth action by employers to facilitate a return to work was conducted in 1972-73, James et al (1997) suggest that the situation has not changed much since that study (Martin and Roberts, 1975): in only 10 – 19% of cases had the employer suggested something to facilitate their return to work.

In our consultation some people questioned whether the development of written policies reflected a serious interest on the part of employing organisations in taking action to retain employees who become disabled while in their employment. A report of an independent postal questionnaire survey of human resource professionals in 77 public and private sector organisations details the return-to-work options provided to employees who were fit to return to work but could not work to their full capacity (Cunningham and James, 1998: forthcoming). Nine out of 10 employees were given adjustments to working hours or a transfer to other work, while almost three quarters were moved to light duties. Cunningham and James point to the need for detailed case study research to explore the "dynamic interplay between the organisational and individual factors which influence the operation of return-to-work activities". Qualitative research might explore how far the different types of employer provision meets the perceived needs of people who become disabled.

A small number of large companies are publicising their approaches to supporting staff who become disabled in order to encourage the spread of good practice.

The Disability Leave initiative arose out of research conducted by the RNIB which had identified the problem that employees who lose their sight discover after they left their jobs that, with special equipment and training, they could have continued working. This was believed to apply also to employees who became disabled in other ways. An evaluation of the operation of the two-year pilot study was based on the experiences and views of 18 employers (including six local authorities and four private sector organisations). Ten of those had adopted, or were already running, an employee-retention

policy. The report (Paschkes-Bell et al, 1996) reproduces an internal study carried out by one piloting employer of the cost and savings of implementing disability leave.

Issues raised by the Disability Leave research include the merits of having a written policy (to avoid both inconsistency and time costs in making decisions on a case-by-case basis) which nonetheless allows flexibility; the need to identify a nominated member of staff responsible for implementing the policy; whether or not to pay the employee all or part of their salary during the period of leave; insurance; and budgeting. The research also identified the need to prepare the ground for implementation of an employment retention policy, and to publicise the policy effectively so that employees to whom it applied were aware of it.

Private insurers have been cited as possible future players in promoting retention of people who become disabled when in work.

UNUM, a supplier of long-term disability insurance, provides a rehabilitation counselling service by medically qualified disability counsellors who focus on early invention strategies looking at personal, medical and occupational circumstances. They review and advise on disability benefits and allowances and determine what type, if any, of rehabilitative help is needed to assist job retention or return to work.

Post Office Disability Advice Centre

The Post Office Disability Advice Centre is a service that provides help and support to staff who become disabled as well as assistance with problems met by staff who are already disabled. This resource provides technological solutions and help to return to the original job or to find an alternative opportunity within the Post Office.

Disability Leave

Disability Leave , a voluntary initiative in partnership with employers, offer a work break for employees who become disabled. It advocates an assessment of the difficulties that a newly disabled person faces in work, poses solutions and a time for reflection before any long-term decisions are made, and enables a newly disabled person to be off work while adjustments are considered and implemented. It supposes that disability leave should be part of an overall employee retention policy. If the employee needs to be away from work to adjust to the disability while adaptations are being made, time should be offered not as sick leave but as disability leave.

Services to support people who become disabled in work

Around half of all employees work in companies with occupational health professionals on site, although provision varies greatly according to the size of the firm (Bunt, 1993, cited in James et al, 1997). However, there is little research evidence to suggest that occupational health professionals play an active part in helping workers to keep their jobs when they become disabled. Some of those we consulted thought that their role deserved detailed research investigation.

In general, workers who become disabled and their employers have to rely on the public Disability Service and in particular on the services of PACTs, DEAs and, where appropriate, AtW. Lack of knowledge of their availability is widely reported, and there is a general perception of these services as being concerned with obtaining, rather than retaining, employment (Reynolds et al, 1997), although helping people who become disabled to retain their job, and supporting their employer in doing so, is one of the formal aims of PACTs. An autumn 1996 survey of PACT clients and services, commissioned by the ES, found that only a minority of clients may have used PACTs to support job retention: at the time of their PACT assessment 13% were in full-time work and 5% in part-time work (Beinart, 1997).

AtW mainly helps people who already have jobs, although the scheme was originally introduced to promote entry and return to employment of unemployed disabled people. A report on some of the experiences of the first year of AtW by a monitoring group of disability organisations suggested that not enough was being done to raise awareness among employers and employees themselves of the support it could provide if someone becomes disabled while in a job (RNIB/RADAR, 1995).

In addition, there are several hundred independent services which could provide support for job retention. The complexity of service provision is thought by the EFD to create confusion and low take-up among employers.

The problem is not so much the lack of services which could support job retention as the difficulty of orienting them in that direction. Publicly-funded services such as the Supported Employment Scheme have been reported to support some people who become disabled (CRG, 1996), and there is no formal obstacle to doing so. While some independent organisations may well wish to respond to this emerging market, they are dependent on funding structures in which PACTs, TECs, local authorities and European sources determine the services needed. It is here that development projects could be encouraged.

The experience of using support services

There are a small number of accounts by disabled people who have become visually impaired while in work of their experiences of using AtW and other services provided by voluntary organisations (for example Glickman, 1996). These stories provide powerful evidence of delays and lack of coordination in provision of equipment which obstruct early resumption of work. Some respondents to our consultation argued for more qualitative research on the experience of using such services.

Development projects

RNIB stands out as a voluntary organisation with a long-standing interest in services to support job retention. Some organisations representing the interests of, and providing services for, people with mental health problems are now turning their attention to job retention. Mind hopes to take forward, in partnership with

REHAB UK

REHAB UK has launched the Get Back project with the dual aim of developing a system of early intervention and support for workers who become disabled and developing return-to-work policies and procedures for employers. This is to include a direct service covering home visits, individual assessment and work-site assessment, as well as work with employers to increase their understanding of what it means for the person returning to work.

employers, the idea of 'job buddies' for people who have mental health problems. Some people we consulted pointed to the need for sympathetic working arrangements which 'allow' people to be ill while on the job.

It is clear that the development of support to help people to stay in employment needs the involvement of all stakeholders. So far, partnerships between employers and the voluntary sector are being taken forward, but disabled people are not key actors in the development and implementation of projects. It is hoped that the new round of HORIZON projects, the National Disability Development Initiative launched by the ES and the Welfare to Work project funding recently announced will redress the imbalance.

Part Three
Future research and development

A changing agenda

"We have got a reasonable under-standing of the spread of the barriers but we have to keep updating that and be aware of them, but then what follows on from that is how do we tackle the barriers? That is the next step in the re-search, practical ways, and help for employers to know what to do, who they need to be working through, all the buzz words like partnership and synergy and so on, we need to know how to do these things and tell other people how to do these things."

"There's been masses done on the old research agenda, but now we need to know about new things ... having an influence on what's coming up rather than what's already happened."

In Part Two we concentrated on the views of disabled people themselves. In this final section of the review, we turn towards the community of research users as a whole including disabled people and their organisations, employers, service providers and a range of stakeholders. As the two quotations above illustrate, our consultation revealed some divergence of views between those who felt it important to keep a focus on the 'moving target' of barriers to the employment of disabled people, and those who felt that it was time for research to move into new areas. We invited representatives of the various interests involved to a seminar at which priorities for future research were discussed. The quotations below reflect a wide range of perspectives and include the voices of both disabled and non-disabled people.

Who asks the questions and who needs to know?

Disabled people are not themselves currently involved in a great deal of research into disability and employment, whether as researchers, commissioners or funders. Nor are they much involved in the design, development or evaluation of the services they use. The concept of user involvement, which has become increasingly important in community care services, is based on the assumption that people need both a means of expressing their preferences and the power to ensure that these preferences are put into action before they can exert control over their daily lives. This would imply that a new agenda for disability research should be framed by disabled people themselves. Our review has sought the ideas of disabled people specifically to shape the research agenda, but enabling disabled people to control research lies ultimately with the funders. Such a concept would represent a major shift in the thinking of, for instance, the DfEE.

It is important to realise that, quite apart from neglecting the views of disabled people, research has not always served other audiences well, either.

"So much research is out of touch with the needs of people who want to effect change. It needs to be oriented towards the needs of employers."

"What do policy makers need to know about the disability dimension in order to improve the quality of life for disabled people?"

It has been argued that employers who want to recruit disabled people also experience barriers, for instance the fact that disabled people may find it difficult to attend careers fairs at which employers meet potential applicants.

> "Let's recognise the common problem and all work together on it, get people talking to each other."

Meeting the needs of employers and disabled people

Findings from research need to be carefully tailored to the people who can carry them forward. Everyone needs to be at the table – disabled people, employers, funders, provider organisations, insurers, and all those with a stake in the outcomes. Although many employers may have resisted change, they need to be brought on board.

> "If it doesn't work for the employer, it won't work at all!"

Employers are notoriously reluctant to take part in research for a number of reasons. One is the pressure to be seen to be doing and saying the right things in an area which is highly charged politically. Another problem is that disabled people and employers perceive a different set of issues.

> "When you talk to employers very few of the barriers which disabled people have mentioned over the years – which they have been concerned about – come up for them [the employers]."

> "A solution which works for employers may not be best for the disabled person."

Although real conflicts of interest can exist between disabled people and employers, these are not radically different from the potential conflicts of interest between any employer and employee. The task for research and development practice is to identify the 'overlapping core' of interests and to frame research questions in such a way that they are perceived as joint problems to which a 'win–win' solution can be found.

It is important for research to recognise that employers are not monoliths but a series of

individual managers, who need to see benefits from equal opportunities practice in their own designated areas of work. The picture of employer practice needs to be derived from a representative cross-section, rather than being distorted by examples of good practice by 'flagship' employers. Lessons can be learnt from an examination by employers themselves if their management styles and practices.

The disabled person as an 'ordinary worker'

The need to confront stereotypical views held by employers emerged as an important strand in discussion. Perceptions about costs, for instance, are often based on misguided notions of the types of workplace adjustments which are required.

> "Technology doesn't mean something like Stephen Hawking has!"

> "Adjustments are often just ordinary things you would do for any worker."

> "Everyone needs their needs meeting in the workplace. The 'mentally healthy workplace' can be just as important as talking about discrimination explicitly."

This can only be helped by the inclusion of disability as one strand in research about employment generally.

The balance of research

The type and amount of research carried out at present is not related to the priorities of disabled people, the needs of employers, or to the relative importance of different issues. Instead it is dominated by funding structures and the evaluation of existing provision. The review identified four critical imbalances.

A concentration on certain groups and neglect of others

We have repeatedly noted the impairment-specific bias in research and provision. People with mental health problems and people with learning disabilities have received much research attention, although (or perhaps because) their needs are often thought to be neglected in the provision of employment services. Interest groups continue to call for their members' needs to be reflected in research, and criteria for national and European funded initiatives continue to specify coverage by impairment.

Very little research and development work has focused on the employment situation and experiences of disabled people who are women or are from minority ethnic groups. Younger disabled people appear to receive more attention than older people because of the practical emphasis on training and preparation for employment. Little is known about the employment needs of disabled people in rural areas. Research could be framed in such a way as to look at common experiences among those who have never worked, those who have had multiple spells of unemployment, those who choose to work part time, and so on.

For many people, disability is only one element in a complex interaction of factors, including age, gender, ethnicity, impairment, occupation and family circumstance.

> "The experience of a young Afro-Caribbean lone mother with sickle cell disease is going to be quite different from that of a Bangladeshi ex-foundry worker with a quite different set of impairments."

As with the broader concept of social exclusion, this interaction makes it hard to understand the dynamics which are at work. Employers may not necessarily see disability as the main thing (although in work of this kind everyone assumes that it is the most important factor) and may possibly discriminate on grounds of long-term unemployment rather than disability. To answer these questions we need

> "... research and development projects which get inside the heads of people who are appointing – to encourage them to employ disabled people in the same way as everyone else."

A focus on the need for change on the part of the disabled person rather than employers

In both research and development, action directed at getting people to change to meet organisational needs is emphasised more than organisations changing themselves.

> "It's the organisation that has to change, not the individual. That's the whole point about equal opportunities and equality of access. People still think it's about the individual getting qualifications, getting the confidence, getting the housing sorted out, getting their transport sorted out – it's not seen as corporate responsibility."

On the other hand, there is a lack of attention to the disabling barriers within employing organisations and a real need for

> "... research on systemic physical and social barriers, to help plan for systemic organisational change rather than the individualistic approach."

An emphasis on training and entering work

The great majority of practical projects and much of the research effort is directed towards preparation for and access to work, but is typically limited to specific points in the pathway into work rather than exploring the whole process of obtaining employment. Fundamental research is needed to understand why disabled people are not applying for jobs.

> "Despite going out and talking to people, working through community groups, all that sort of thing, people still don't believe that they are going to end up with a job."

The number of people becoming disabled in post exceeds the number of disabled people trying to get into work, yet this area is under-researched, as is the experience of working as a disabled person. Older disabled people with a history of work are particularly neglected in research and development.

A tendency to approach the employment of disabled people as a question of evaluating specialist provision

Many research studies consist of evaluations of specific schemes and projects for disabled people. But disabled people wondered if some of these projects might have done more harm than good, by labelling them as a group with special needs.

> "We've got all these specialist workers and specialist routes into things and people try on our behalf to persuade employers to take us – maybe that approach has done us more of a disservice."

It was suggested that research might fruitfully:

- look at what is wrong with the mainstream ways of getting people into work, how people in general get jobs and what needs to change;

- track labour market experience to spot where disabled people fall out of the mainstream and why;

- identify the features of projects which do work.

At the same time, it was argued that segregated employment should not be dismissed, as it was meeting the specific needs of some disabled people.

What are the questions that need to be answered?

Do we know enough about barriers already?

We were warned (by non-disabled people) against more research which just confirms the existence of problems, without doing anything to resolve them. But for some people, in some circumstances, barriers have not been explored enough:

- discrimination and people with 'new' impairments (ME, HIV) or people with chronic conditions like back pain who are not thought to be 'really' disabled. This latter group make up the largest group of people with a long-term disability, yet are almost invisible in both research and development initiatives;

- prejudice about the sort of work which disabled people are thought capable of doing (as legitimised by 'excluded occupations' in the DDA);

- prejudice about what 'work' is; for instance is voluntary work a legitimate alternative to paid employment? Why are careers in the arts not seen as 'proper jobs'?;

- impairment-related barriers may be an important area;

> "There needs to be a really nuts and bolts understanding of how the barriers impact on people with different impairments if these barriers are to be addressed and put right. Barriers which can operate at a quite unconscious level."

but

> "There are too many people picking on people's impairments and comparing impairments, not comparing barriers. The common experience is discrimination."

- the barriers within the workplace, including colleagues' attitudes and behaviour.

In sum,

> "It's crazy to say we don't need to do more research on the subtleties of barriers, as there is so little – we have hardly begun."

The changing barriers

There is often confusion about the concept of 'barriers', which tends to be used as a portmanteau word for all the problems confronting disabled people. There are, in fact, several analytically distinct issues, which require different types of approaches:

- barriers facing individuals (albeit resulting from structural barriers such as segregated education or the benefits system) which can be overcome by assistance along the way (for example, training to present oneself at interview) – much of the activity we identified was of this type;

- barriers which could be reduced or removed by making the system more efficient (for example, by making service delivery more responsive to individual need – or delivering equipment more quickly);

- the barriers created by the behaviour of most non-disabled people which can be tackled by legislation, disability equality training and education;

- structural, or institutional, barriers.

Attempts to reduce and remove barriers may merely change them.

> "The introduction of the DDA has simply changed the nature of some of barriers."

More subtle forms of discrimination may take the place of the more blatant; for example, disabled people may be put under pressure to leave work 'voluntarily'. It is important, therefore, to look at the changing configuration of barriers and not assume that action has successfully 'removed' them.

An unmet need for facts and figures

Despite the existence of survey data, many information needs are still not being satisfied.

> "Different organisations use different definitions – people are talking about different things but the figures are lumped together – for people working on disability projects there is a strong need for accurate, reliable figures."

> "Working on the retention of newly disabled people – I can't evaluate my project because the baseline information is not there. Employers either don't have or won't show this information."

Information needs include data on the employment of disabled people by sector and by size of enterprise; barriers will differ depending on the type of trade or industry and between small, medium-sized and large organisations.

It was also argued that there was a need for more sophisticated work to cost interventions in relation to outcomes, especially in relation to the government's New Deal programme.

How to answer the questions

Research needs to use methods which not only enable the voices of disabled people to be

heard, but provide tangible results, that is, emancipatory research methods and action research which is geared to positive outcomes for the participants.

The need for experiential research which captures the disabled person's perspective – particularly the experience of being in work – was highlighted by a number of contributors. But research should not be limited to the experiences of disabled people. Asking non-disabled people about their experience of working (including working with disabled people) could be just as illuminating and might lessen the acknowledged ethical and practical difficulties of exploring disabled people's experiences within the workplace.

There was also felt to be a need for research which can provide information on a lifetime's experience, rather than reporting on a single moment in time, for example, longitudinal surveys which 'track' the employment experience of disabled people. Transitions – notably from school – could be explored, and the experiences of disabled and non-disabled young people compared.

One strand which emerged quite strongly was the need for research to identify the ways in which disabled people had overcome difficulties and achieved success. Issues for further research include:

- strategies and strengths of disabled people;

- success in a business environment, not in the 'safety' of a 'disability' job;

- disseminating information about what has worked in terms of helping disabled people obtain or remain in work.

New areas for research

Throughout this report we have pointed to gaps in the research and suggested questions for further research and development. In developing an agenda we have also identified some emerging trends which might be examined.

The professionalisation of disability

- disability as a qualification for the job;

- disabled people working or setting up in disability-specific organisations;

- the 'knock-on' effects in terms of changing attitudes – among users, other workers, employers, disabled children and young people;

- the pressures on people who take on these jobs or who act as role models.

The impact of the changing labour market

- the experiences of disabled people on short-term contracts;

- the role of employment agencies;

- the responsiveness of employment services to the changing labour market;

- what voluntary and third-sector work can offer.

The impact of voluntary employment policies

- how policies actually operate in employing organisations – how does equal opportunities policy 'filter through' an organisation?

- the impact of the 'business case' – what do employers really think and what are the views of disabled employees?

- are there real differences between a 'managing diversity' and 'equal opportunities' perspective?

- can large employers have an influence through contract requirements?

Financial incentives to employers

- the effects of the New Deal and competition between 'disadvantaged groups' in a subsidised labour market;

- how funding can be tied to achievement of real jobs which last.

Practical research

The review identified a need for the huge variety of development initiatives which exist to be more effectively targeted, more systematically evaluated, and brought to the

attention of a much wider audience. Issues include:

- the need to consult employers, as well as disabled people, when designing projects;

- projects linked to the employer, so that employers actually take some responsibility;

- how to build on success by advancing projects beyond the pilot stage;

- the need for a directory mapping the range of projects, and their outcomes;

- what is good practice?

Many research evaluations look at a single initiative. This is problematic, as it is not possible to identify which, if any, aspects of a successful initiative might usefully be replicated elsewhere, and which are the result of a combination of factors which is unique to that project. There is a need for development projects which are undertaken and evaluated as a linked whole, so that genuinely effective strategies for future work can be demonstrated.

Research that makes a difference

Research does not exist in a vacuum. Implementing good practice means taking account of the other barriers which may exist.

> "There's no point in setting up a new training project if people are totally discouraged by all the other things that are going on around them."

Effective research and development also needs to have a realistic grasp of both the opportunities and the limits to change, for instance with regard to the changing labour market, or the power relationships between employers and disabled people.

Where the creation and demise of occupations and jobs is, for the most part, dependent on market forces it is difficult to see how government agencies can effect the creation of 'new stable jobs' for people with disabilities outside the sphere of sheltered employment. These difficulties are compounded where there is a declared intention of allowing market forces to

determine the demand for labour.
(Moreton, 1992, p 81)

Hyde (1998) makes the same point in looking at the barriers to open employment of disabled people, emphasising the need for legislative rights as a balance to market forces.

Employers will not consent to 'be researched' without evidence of a tangible pay-off for them. This attitude is increasingly shared both by disabled people who are frustrated at being endlessly 'mined' for information, and by hard-pressed provider organisations.

> "What will we get out of doing this for you? Why is it worth my time?"

Factors working against the implementation of a future research agenda include lack of information, lack of trust and an atmosphere of competition both within and between research and provider organisations. These can be overcome by the development of new working methods. One example given at the seminar was that of a long-standing discussion group involving professionals from a variety of disciplines. Crucial to the success of this initiative was that it was not tied to a particular venue, so that all of those involved felt that they shared 'ownership' of the group.

The DDA was cited as one positive influence on the current climate. For organisations, employment issues and service delivery may be linked. Improving service delivery to disabled people may create an impetus to deal with employment. For instance, Deafworks, an organisation offering consultancy and training

services, is carrying out work with a local authority on how to implement the DDA in respect of Deaf people, which will deal both with service delivery and employment. Such good practice is by no means automatic; the example was given of theatres which have improved access for the public but not for employees behind the scenes (Arts Council of Great Britain, 1993).

The £195m currently available for projects under the New Deal, and the policy emphasis on reducing social security expenditure, both create an impetus to the creation of projects and a rationale for evaluating their outcomes. New methods, involving partnerships between employers, providers and disabled people are a requirement for development projects to be established under the New Deal.

Those who took part in the review were positive about the role of research in improving the opportunities for disabled people to work. But they were also aware of the shortcomings of some existing research, which has too often failed to translate into changes in practice. This is partly a question for research itself – its content, methodology and orientation – but it is also an issue about the overall role of research in influencing the policy process. There is currently some evidence of political will to change the employment situation of disabled people. The various stakeholders – disabled people, employers, providers – will need to maintain an ongoing dialogue with both government and with the major commissioners of research about the types of policies – and the types of research – they require.

References

Abberley, P. (1992) 'Counting us out: a discussion of the OPCS disability surveys', *Disability, Handicap & Society*, vol 7, no 2, pp 139-55.

Arber, S. (1991) 'Class, paid employment and family roles: making sense of structural disadvantage, gender and health status', *Social Science and Medicine*, vol 32, pp 425-36.

Arts Council of Great Britain (1993) *Report on the initiative to increase the employment of disabled people in the arts*, London: Arts Council of Great Britain.

Barnes, C. (1991) *Disabled people in Britain and discrimination: A case for anti-discriminatory legislation*, London: Hurst and Co/University of Calgary Press.

Bass, M. and Drewett, R. (1997) *Supported employment for people with learning difficulties*, Joint Unit for Social Sciences Research, Sheffield University.

Beinart, S. (1997) *A survey of PACT clients and services*, London: Social and Community Planning Research.

Beinart, S., Smith, P. and Sproston, K. (1996) *The Access to Work programme: A survey of recipients, employers, Employment Service managers and staff*, London: Social and Community Planning Research.

Berthoud, R., Lakey, J. and McKay, S. (1993) *The economic problems of disabled people*, London: PSI.

Bolderson, H. and Youll, P. with Gains, F. and Tarpey, M. (1997) 'Participation in the Third European Action Programme for Handicapped People Living Independently in an Open Society (HELIOS II): An evaluation of the United Kingdom's experience', Report to the DoH, London, Brunel University.

Busby, P. (1991) 'Report on problems faced by people with disabilities entering self-employment', Stoke-on-Trent Staffordshire TEC.

Collings, J. and Chappell, B. (1994) 'Correlates of employment history and employability in a British epilepsy sample', *Seizure*, no 3, pp 255-62.

Cooper, M. (1992) *Employers' attitudes*, Leeds: British Epilepsy Association.

Corden, A. (1997) *Supported employment, people and money*, Social Policy Report No 7, York: Social Policy Research Unit.

Corden, A. and Thornton, P. (1997) 'Case studies on employment of people with disabilities in small and medium-sized enterprises: UK', Working Paper WP/97/56/EN, Dublin: European Foundation for the Improvement of Living and Working Conditions.

Cornell, L. (1997a) *Make your experience count Book 1 – Recognising ability*, Learning from Experience Trust, Chelmsford: Anglia Polytechnic University.

Cornell, L. (1997b) *Make your experience count Book 2 – Demonstrating ability*, Learning from Experience Trust, Chelmsford: Anglia Polytechnic University.

Cornell, L. (1997c) *Recognising ability project final report*, Learning from Experience Trust, Chelmsford: Anglia Polytechnic University.

Cornes, P. (1994) 'Learning difficulties and work: the search for new initiatives', *REHAB Network*, Spring, 15-17.

Coulson, R. (1997) 'Perspectives and retrospectives – CHOICE Report 2', Gillingham: CHOICE.

CPAG (Child Poverty Action Group) (1997/98) *Rights guide to non-means-tested benefits*, London: CPAG.

CRG Research Consultancy Training (1996) 'Focus groups report: A review of contractual arrangements for supported employment', Report submitted to the ES, December 1996.

Cunningham, I. (1993) *Disability and employment*, Stockton-on-Tees: Jim Conway Foundation.

Cunningham, I. and James, P. (1998: forthcoming) 'Absence and return to work: towards a research agenda', *Personnel Review*.

CVS Consultants/GLAD (Greater London Associaton of Disabled People) (1997) *Ethnicity and disability: Moving towards equity in service provision*, London: CVS Consultants.

Darr, A., Jones, L., Ahmad, W. and Nisar, G. (1997) *A directory of projects and initiatives with deaf people from ethnic minorities*, Bradford/York: Ethnicity and Social Policy Research Unit, University of Bradford/Social Policy Research Unit, University of York.

Davoud, N. (1980) *Part-time employment: Time for recognition, organisation and legal reform*, London: RADAR/Multiple Sclerosis Society.

Deafworks (1997) *Deaf arts audit: Research into the provision of arts activities for deaf people in England*, London: Arts Council of England.

De Caro, J., Evans, L. and Dowaliby, F. (1982) 'Advising deaf youth to train for various occupations', *British Journal of Educational Psychology*, no 52, pp 220-7.

Delany, L. (1998) 'Prejudice in the small firm', *New Law Journal*, no 148, pp 27-8.

Dench, S., Meager, N. and Morris, S. (1996) *The recruitment and retention of people with disabilities*, Institute for Employment Studies Report 301, Brighton: Institute for Employment Studies, University of Sussex.

DfEE (Department for Education and Employment) (1997) *Making a difference: A good practice guide for employers' networks on disability*, London: HMSO.

Dick, N. and Shepherd, G. (1994) 'Work and mental health: a preliminary test of Warr's model in sheltered workshops for the mentally ill', *Journal of Mental Health*, no 3, pp 387-400.

Di Terlizzi, M. (1997) 'Talking about work: I used to talk about nothing else, I was excited and it got a bit too much for my parents', *Disability & Society*, vol 12, no 4, pp 501-11.

DRT (Disability Resource Team) (1994) 'Good practice in employment', London: DRT.

DSS (Department of Social Security) (1997) *Directory of disability information sources*, DSS in-house Report 31, London: Analytical Services Division, DSS.

Eardley, T. and Corden, A. (1996) *Low income self-employment: Work, benefits and living standards*, Aldershot: Avebury.

EOR (Equal Opportunities Review) (1997) 'Implementing the DDA: an EOR survey of employers', *Equal Opportunities Review*, vol 71, January/February.

Erens, B. and Ghate, D. (1993) *Invalidity Benefit: A longitudinal survey of new recipients*, DSS Research Report No 20, London: HMSO.

Erne, C. (1991) *Employment of disabled people in local authorities: A three year project to promote the employment of disabled people in six local authorities*, London: RADAR.

ES (Employment Service) (1990) *Evaluation of special schemes for people with disabilities: Summary paper*, Sheffield: ES.

European Commission (1996) *HELIOS II European guide to good practice: Towards equal opportunities for disabled people*, Luxembourg: Office for Official Publications of the European Communities.

European Commission (1997) *Better employment opportunities for people with disabilities*, The Employment–HORIZON Initiative, Special Report, Brussels: DGV, European Social Fund.

Fagin, L. and Little, M. (1984) *The forsaken families: The effects of unemployment on family life*, Harmondsworth: Penguin Books.

Floyd, M. (1995) 'Self employment and disabled people in the United Kingdom', *International Journal of Practical Approaches to Disability*, vol 19, no 2, pp 9-14.

French, S. (1988) *'They weren't obstructive, but they didn't go out of their way to be helpful either' – Disabled people in the health and caring professions: professional attitudes and personal experiences*, Health and Social Services Research Unit Research Paper 2, London: South Bank Polytechnic.

French, S. (1995) 'Visually impaired physiotherapists: their struggle for acceptance and survival', *Disability & Society*, vol 10, no 1, pp 3-20.

Garforth, A. (1997) *DATA 2000 – the way forward*, Bradford: DATA.

Glickman, M. (1996) 'Disability and the cost-minimising imperative: a personal evaluation of being a PACT team client', *REHAB Network*, Autumn, pp 15-19.

Graham, P., Jordon, A. and Lamb, B. (1990) *An equal chance? Or no chance? A study of discrimination against disabled people in the labour market*, London: The Spastics Society.

Grove, G., Freudenberg, M., Harding, A. and O'Flynn, D. (1997) *The social firm handbook: New directions in the employment, rehabilitation and integration of people with mental health problems*, Brighton: Pavilion.

Handy, C. (1994) *The empty raincoat: Making sense of the future*, London: Hutchinson.

Hirst, M. and Baldwin, S. (1994) *Unequal opportunities: Growing up disabled*, London: HMSO.

Home Office (1995) 'Make a difference: An outline volunteering strategy for the UK', London: Home Office.

Honey, S., Meager, N. and Williams, M. (1993) *Employers' attitudes towards people with disabilities*, Employment Department Research Brief, Sheffield: Employment Department.

HOP (Home Office Partnership) (1997) 'COMBAT: Corporate marketing to overcome the barriers facing disabled teleworkers', Research Summary, Cambridge: HOP.

Hyde, M. (1996) 'Fifty years of failure: employment services for disabled people in the UK', *Work, Employment & Society*, vol 10, no 4, pp 683-700.

Hyde, M. (1998) 'Sheltered and supported employment in the 1990s: the experiences of disabled workers in the UK', *Disability & Society*, vol 13, no 2, pp 199–216.

Hyde, M. and Howes, J. (1993) *Disability and employment in Devon: Into the 1990s*, Exeter: Devon Committee for the Employment of People with Disabilities.

Industrial Society (1995) *Managing diversity*, Managing Best Practice No 14, London: The Industrial Society.

Jahoda, M. (1982) *Employment and unemployment: A social–psychological analysis*, Cambridge: Cambridge University Press.

James, P., Bruyère, S. and Cunningham, I. (1997) 'Absence and disability management', *Review of Employment Topics*, vol 5, no 1, pp 152-85.

Jamison, J. (1995) 'Visually impaired candidates for employment', London: Blind in Business.

JRF (Joseph Rowntree Foundation) (1996) 'Deaf people's participation in local services', Findings, Social Care Research 77, York: JRF.

Kelvin, P. and Jarrett, J. (1985) *Unemployment – its social–psychological effects*, Cambridge: Cambridge University Press.

Kestenbaum, A. (1996) *Independent Living: A review*, York: York Publishing Services for JRF.

Kettle, M. (1979) *Disabled people and their employment: A review of research into the performance of disabled people at work*, London: RADAR/Association of Disabled Professionals.

Kingston JCAG (Joint Commissioning Advisory Group for People with a Learning Disability) (1997) 'Just the job: Report on the findings of the Employment and Training Sub-Group', Kingston: Royal Borough of Kingston upon Thames.

Kyle, J., Thomas, C. and Pullen, G. (1989) 'Assessing deaf people for employment and rehabilitation: Project report', Bristol: Centre for Deaf Studies, University of Bristol.

Laurie, L. and Higgins, M. (undated) *Working together for our equality*, Western TEC.

Lunt, N. and Thornton, P. (1994) 'Disability and employment: towards an understanding of discourse and policy', *Disability & Society*, vol 9, no 2, pp 223-38.

MacFarlane, R. (1997) *Unshackling the poor*, York: York Publishing Services.

Maginn, A. and Meager, N. (1995) *Local employer networks on disability: Summary report*, Brighton: Institute of Employment Studies.

Manning, C. and White, P. (1995) 'Attitudes of employers to the mentally ill', *Psychiatric Bulletin*, no 19, pp 541-3.

Martin, J., Meltzer, H. and Elliot, D. (1988) *The prevalence of disability among adults*, London: HMSO.

Mason, M. and Reiser, R. (1990) *Disability equality in the classroom: A human rights issue*, London: Disability Equality in Education.

Maynard Campbell, S. and Smyth, K. (1998) *Disabled people into employment: The report of a UK-wide survey of good practice in projects with disabled people and employment informing ideas for the development of a strategic framework for action*, Nottingham: Nottingham City Council/Greater Nottingham TEC/ES.

McLaughlin, E. (1994) *Flexibility in work and benefits*, Commission on Social Justice Paper 11, London: Institute for Public Policy Research.

Meager, N. (1995) *'Winners and losers' – Funding issues for the training of people with special training needs*, Report 298, Brighton: Institute of Employment Studies.

Moffett, J., Richardson, G., Sheldon, T. and Maynard, A. (1995) *Back pain – its management and cost to society*, Discussion Paper 129, York: Centre for Health Economics.

Moon, P. (1990) 'Nurses survey: A survey of twelve nurse members of the Association of Disabled Professionals', London: RADAR.

Moreton, T. (1992) 'European support for people with disabilities', *Personnel Review*, vol 21, no 6, pp 74-87.

Morrell, J. (1990) *The employment of people with disabilities: Research into the policies and practices of employers*, Department of Employment Research Paper No 77, London: Employment Department.

Morris, J. (1994) *The shape of things to come? User-led social services*, Social Policy Forum Paper No 3, London: National Institute for Social Work.

Niyazi, F. (1996) *Volunteering by people with disabilities: A route to opportunity*, London: National Centre for Volunteering.

Nodder, R. (1993) 'Working as a psychologist in the Employment Service – Disability', *Occupational Psychologist*, no 21, pp 18-20.

O'Hare, C. and Thompson, D. (1991) 'Experiences of physiotherapists with physical disabilities', *Physiotherapist*, vol 77, no 6, pp 374-8.

Oliver, M. (1990) *The politics of disablement*, London: Macmillan.

OUTSET (1990) 'Education, training and services for visually impaired people: Study commissioned by London Association for the Blind', London: OUTSET.

Parkinson, M. (1996) 'Accessible training: Improving access to training for disabled trainees – 1996 update with the Essex perspective', Chelmsford: Essex Returners' Unit.

Parkinson, M. and Freeney, M. (1997) 'Disabilities and Employment Conference report and recommendations', London: Focus Central London.

Parr, S., Byng, S. and Gilpin, S. (1997) *Talking about aphasia: Living with loss of language after a stroke*, Milton Keynes: Open University Press.

Paschkes-Bell, G. (1997) 'Visible improvement', *People Management*, 5 December, pp 30-2.

Paschkes-Bell, G., Da Cunha, S. and Hurry, J. (1996) *Adapting to change: When an employee becomes disabled*, London: RNIB.

Perkins, R., Buckfield, R. and Choy, D. (1997) 'Access to employment: a supported employment project to enable mental health service users to obtain jobs within mental health teams', *Journal of Mental Health*, vol 6, no 3, pp 307-18.

Pickvance, S. (1997) 'Employers liability – a system off balance?', *Occupational Health Review*, September-October, pp 1-4.

Pozner, A., M.-L., Ng, Hammond, H. and Shepherd, G. (1996) *Working it out: Creating work opportunities for people with mental health problems, A development handbook*, Brighton: Pavilion.

Prescott-Clarke, P. (1990) *Employment and handicap*, London: Social and Community Planning Research.

PSI/DRUL (Policy Studies Institute/Disability Research Unit, Leeds) (1995) *Measuring disablement in society*, Progress Report 1, London: PSI.

Ravaud, J., Madiot, B. and Ville, I. (1992) 'Discrimination towards disabled people seeking employment', *Social Science and Medicine*, vol 35, no 8, pp 951-8.

Read, J. and Baker, S. (1996) *Not just sticks and stones: A survey of the stigma, taboos, and discrimination experienced by people with mental health problems*, London: Mind.

Reilly, G. (1994) 'Tendring's turn: Pilot investigation of care needs of people with physical disabilities aged 18-64', Essex Physical Disability Joint Planning Team.

Reynolds, G. and Alferoff, C. with Nicholls, P. (1997) *Disabled people and employment in Staffordshire: A study commissioned by Staffordshire County Council*, Staffordshire University.

Rickell, S. (1994) *Working through barriers: A report by Swindon Living Options and The Spastics Society for the Employment Service and Wiltshire Committee for the Employment of Disabled People*, London: The Spastics Society.

Rickell, S. (1997) 'Welcome in work', Somerset County Council.

RNIB/RADAR (1995) 'Access to equality: An analysis of the effectiveness of the Access to Work scheme', London: RNIB/RADAR.

Rolfe, H., Bryson, A. and Metcalfe, H. (1996) *The effectiveness of TECs in achieving jobs and qualifications for disadvantaged groups*, DfEE Research Studies, London: HMSO.

Roulstone, A. (1998) *Enabling technology: Disabled people, work and new technology*, Milton Keynes: Open University Press.

Rowlingson, K. and Berthoud, R. (1996) *Disability, benefits and employment: An evaluation of Disability Working Allowance*, DSS Research Report No 54, London: The Stationery Office.

Schneider-Ross (1995) 'The Windsor Consultation', London: Employers' Forum on Disability.

Scott-Parker, S. (1998) 'Rights and duties: an employer's perspective' in W. Momm and R. Ransom (eds) 'Disability and Work', *Encyclopaedia of Occupational Health and Safety*, Geneva: ILO.

Shepherd, G. (1989) 'The value of work in the 1980s', *Psychiatric Bulletin*, no 13, pp 231-3.

Shepherd, G. (1997) 'Vocational rehabilitation in psychiatry: an historical perspective', in G. Grove, M. Freudenberg, A. Harding and D. O'Flynn *The social firm handbook: New directions in the employment, rehabilitation and integration of people with mental health problems*, Brighton: Pavilion.

Simons, K. (1998) *Home, work and inclusion: The social policy implications of supported living and employment for people with learning disabilties*, York: York Publishing Services.

Sly, F. (1996) 'Disability and the labour market', *Labour Market Trends*, September, pp 413-24.

Sly, F., Duxberry, R. and Tillsley, C. (1995) 'Disability in the labour market: findings from the Labour Force Survey', *Labour Market Trends*, December, pp 439-59.

Smith, B., Povall, M. and Floyd, M. (1991) *Managing disability at work: Improving practice in organisations*, London: Jessica Kingsley Publishers.

Straughair, S. (1992) *The experience of young people with arthritis*, JRF Social Care Findings No 26, York: JRF.

Surrey County Council (1997) 'Open learning for unemployed people, Report of the project, part funded by the European Social Fund, undertaken in learning centres in Surrey libraries in 1996/97 on behalf of the Surrey Training and Enterprise Council', Woking: Surrey TEC.

Taylor, M. (1998) 'Opportunities for disabled artists in education', London: Arts Council of England.

Thomas, A. (1992) *Working with a disability: Barriers and facilitators*, London: Social and Community Planning Research.

Thornton, P. (1998) International Research Project on Job Retention and Return to Work Strategies for disabled workers: Key issues, Geneva: International Labour Office.

Thornton, P. and Lunt, N. (1995) *Employment for disabled people: Social obligation or individual responsibility?*, Social Policy Reports No 2, York: Social Policy Research Unit, University of York.

Thornton, P. and Lunt, N. (1996) 'Disabled people, work and benefits: a review of the research literature', Paper prepared for a JRF Seminar, 12 November, York: Social Policy Research Unit, University of York.

Thornton, P. and Lunt, N. (1998: forthcoming) 'Working opportunities for disabled people', in J. Wheelock and J. Vail (eds) *Work and idleness: The political economy of full employment*, Boston, MA: Kluwer.

Tillsley, C. (1997) 'Gaining access to employment opportunities', *British Journal of Visual Impairment*, vol 15, no 2, pp 67-71.

Vernon, A. (1996) 'Disabled women in the labour market', Paper to European Conference on Self-determined Living for Disabled Women, Munich, 15-18 August.

Vernon, A. (1997) 'Reflexivity: the dilemmas of researching from the inside', in C. Barnes and G. Mercer (eds) *Doing disability research*, Leeds: Disability Press.

Walsh, K., Berry-Lound, D. and Bysshe, S. (1997) *Interim evaluation of the Employment Community Initiative*, DfEE Research Report No 8, London: DfEE.

Warr, P. (1982) 'Psychological aspects of employment and unemployment', *Psychological Medicine*, no 12, pp 7-11.

Warr, P. (1984) 'Job loss, unemployment and psychological well-being', in V. Allen and E. Van der Vliert (eds) *Role transitions*, New York, NY: Plenum Press.

Warr, P. (1985) 'Twelve questions about unemployment and health', in B. Roberts (ed) *New approaches to economic life*, Manchester: Manchester University Press.

Watson, A., Owen, G., Aubrey, J. and Ellis, B. (1998) *Integrating disabled employees: Case studies of 40 employees*, Research Report No 56, London: DfEE.

Whitfield, G. (1997) *The Disability Discrimination Act: Analysis of data from an Omnibus Survey*, DSS Social Research Branch in-house Report 30, London: DSS.

Wills, G., Madden, P., Khourami, D., Smith, L., Costin, M., French, S. and Green, J. (undated) 'Barriers to employment of disabled people', London: Excel Employment Agency.

Winyard, S. (1996) *Blind in Britain: The employment challenge*, London: RNIB.

Young, A., Ackerman, J. and Kyle, J. (1998) *Looking on: Deaf people and the organisation of services*, Bristol: The Policy Press.

Zahno, K. and Wurr, J. (1996) 'Improving training and employment opportunities for people with physical disabilities and sensory impairments', A report to Bromley Joint Commissioning by CAG Consultants.

Zarb, G. (1997) 'Researching disabled barriers', in C. Barnes and G. Mercer (eds) *Doing disability research*, Leeds: Disability Press.

Zarb, G. and Oliver, M. (1993) *Ageing with a disability: What do they expect after all these years?*, London: University of Greenwich.

Appendix:
Contributors to the review

Madelaine Aitkenhead, Mid-Bedfordshire CVS

Artificial Limb and Appliance Service

Sue Arthur, Policy Studies Institute

Tony Ashwell, DIAL UK

Asian People with Disabilities Alliance

Simone Aspis

Association of Muslims with Disabilities

M. Ballantine

Mary Barbour, Warrington CVS

David Barker, Ability 2000 at Disability North

Zoe Barker, LEODIS

Donna Barnett, Moray Resource Centre

Molly Barrett

Denise Barrows, FOCUS (Central London TEC)

Carol Beattie, Employment Service

Geraldine Begg, East Renfrewshire District Council

Claire Benjamin, Joseph Rowntree Foundation

Catherine Bewley, British Limbless Ex-Servicemen's Association

Carol Borowski, National Federation of the Blind

Dee Boyle, Special Needs Action on Careers

Sharon Bramwell, Nottinghamshire Deaf Society

Andrew Bruce

Marie Burns, Glasgow Association for Mental Health

Helen Burrill

Sue Butterworth, Dialability Oxford

Kate Byrne, Making Space

Mike Calver, Manic Depression Fellowship

L. Frances Campbell, Inverness Access Committee

Grant Carson, Centre for Independent Living, Glasgow

Alden Chadwick, Sheffield City Council

David Chung, Sutton Alliance of Disabled People

Linda Clarke, Spinal Injuries Association

Nick Clarke, Association of Blind and Partially Sighted Teachers and Students

Bec Clarkson, UK Coalition

Alison Cobb, MIND

Alison Coles, Museums and Galleries Commission

Janice Cooper, The Welsh Office

Christine Cooper Lastockin, Worklink

Richard Coulson, CHOICE

Liz Cornell, Learning from Experience Trust

Peter Craig, Department of Social Security

David Crookes, Western Training and Enterprise Council

Felicity Crofts, Cedars Medical Rehabilitation Unit

Brian Davey, Nottingham Advocacy Group

Rhian Davies, Cardiff and Vale Coalition of Disabled People

Ann Davis

Justin Davis Smith, Institute for Volunteering
Research

Nicole Davoud

Linda Delaney, Manchester Metropolitan
University

Derbyshire Coalition of Disabled People

Stephanie Dickinson, Department for Education
and Employment

Michael Dineen

Disability Information Trust

Disjointed Ltd

Linda Dodd, Kent Social Services Department

Anthony Dove, CHASE

Brian Doyle, Liverpool University

Jo Doyle, West of England Centre for
Independent Living

Niamh Doyle

Sheila Durie, Edinburgh Community Trust

Elite Self Employment Agency

Brenda Ellis, GLAD

Richard Exell, Trades Union Congress

Geraldine Ferry, University of York

Leigh Fiorentino, University of Sheffield

Bill Fisher, Lothian Coalition of Disabled People

Mike Floyd, City University

Carl Ford

John Foster, St Helens Careers Service

Tony Foster, Surrey University

Jeff Fowler, Greater Peterborough Disability
Forum

Sally French

Sarah Frost, British Epilepsy Association

Albert Gable, Essex Disabled People's
Association

Max Gallagher, Real Jobs Edinburgh

Peter Gagg, Employment Opportunities for
People with Disabilities

Yvettte Galton

Ian Gardener, National Disability Development
Initiative

Andrew Garforth, DATA

Stuart Garland

Grant Garson, Centre for Independent Living in
Glasgow

Laura Garuti

David Gayter, Staffordshire County Council

Val George, Horticultural Therapy

Lol Gellor, Cultural Partnerships

Mark Gilbert, ECOTEC

Murray Glickman

Selwyn Goldsmith

Caroline Gooding, Trades Union Disability
Alliance

Ruth Gould, Full Circle Arts

Lorraine Gradwell, Breakthrough UK Ltd

Steve Griffiths, Brent Black Carribean Disabled
People's Association

Bob Grove, Richmond Fellowship

David Gunn

Sandra Hanafin, Action for Blind People

Julie Hanks, Mendip District Council

Jenny Hawkes

Ken Hawkin, SCOPE

Rosemarie Harris, Lambeth Accord

Angela Heenan, Employment Service

John Hicks, The Welsh Office

Dione Hills, Tavistock Institute

Julie Hobbs, REHAB UK

Sarah Hodgkinson, Multiple Sclerosis Society
Colchester

Geoffrey Holland

Tim Honnor

Horticultural Therapy

Cath Howard, West Cumbria Carers

Marilyn Howard

John Hughes, St Helens YMCA Foyer

Jane Hunt

Sandra Hutton and colleague, WWIN

Mark Hyde, University of Plymouth

Jon Hyslop, National Schizophrenia Fellowship

Ideas in Motion, Liverpool University

Richard Ibbotson, Scottish Society for Autistic Children

Carol Infanti, Bromley Joint Commissioing

John Innes-Watt

Mike Jackson, Cheshire County Council

Audrey Jacobs, Maidenhead Multiple Sclerosis Society

Elaine James, Disablement Association of Barking and Dagenham

Mark James, Employment Service

Phil James, Black Spectrum

Philip James, Middlesex University

Rachel James

Ann Jappie

Christopher Jeal, Bromley Association for People with Handicaps

Judith Jesky, Cambridge County Council

Howard John, Disability Wales

George Johnson, Conwy Disability Forum

Robert Johnstone

Carolyn Jones, Institute of Employment Rights

Mike Jones

Sali Jones, Cardiff University

Pauline Jones, Disability Advice Project

P.M. Keane, Keane Goodway & Co

David Kelly

John Kelly, Brighton CVS

Kent Social Services

Ann Kestenbaum

King's Fund Library and Information Service

Tim Kleinschmidt, University of Plymouth

Phillip Lacey, Department for Education and Employment

Brian Lamb, SCOPE

Peter Large

Denise Largin, Camden Society for People with Learning Difficulties

Jim Lawson, Employers Network on Disability

Barry Leach, Hull Council of Disabled People

Tim Leach, ASBAH

Freda Levinson

Richard Light

Alison Lord, Causeway, Renfrewshire Association for Mental Health

Colin Low, City University

David MacGeorge, St Loyes College, Exeter

Jim MacLeod

Margaret McDiarmid

Brian McGinnis, MENCAP

Ann and Donald McIntyre

Ian McKee, North Tyneside Coalition of Disabled People

Eamon McLelland, Bath and North East Somerset County Council

Jane McMillan, Shaw Trust

Joy McMillan, Essex Returners Unit

Jeff McWhinney, British Deaf Association

Ian Malcolm Walker, TUDA

Paddy Masefield

Bert Massie, RADAR

Nigel Meager, Institute for Employment Studies

Niall Milligan, Next Step

Raj Mistry, Asian People with Disabilities Alliance

Patrick Molloy, Disability Information Trust

Paddy Moon, Association of Disabled Professionals

Robert Mottram, Disability West Midlands

Joan Nation, Brent Association of Disabled People

National Lottery Charities Board

New Ways to Work

Debbie Nunn, Birmingham Disability Resource Centre

Steve Ogilvie, Kite Employment Service

Geraldine O'Halloran, Greenwich Association of Disabled People

Tony Oliver

Philip Oxley, Cranfield University

Mabel Pakenham-Walsh

Ewart Parkinson, Cardiff Association of the Single Homeless

Ginny Parkes ,Disability Partnership in Essex

Susie Parr, City University

Gillian Paschkes Bell ,Royal National Institute for the Blind

Keith Pattison

Angela Payne ,Surrey Training and Enterprise Council

John Perry, Henshaw Society for the Blind

Christine Pickthall, Vale Royal Disability Services

Janet Pollard, Worklink

Adam Pozner, OUTSET Consultancy

Jinny Purkis, Essex County Council

QEST, Cambridge

Ann Rae

Jean-François Ravaud, Institut Fédératif de Recherche sur le Handicap

Margaret Read, CMT International UK

Paul Redfern, Deafworks

Gerard Reilly, Tendring DIAL

Josée van Remoortel, World Federation for Mental Health

Bill Riddell

Julie Ridley

Vivian Rivlin

Damien Robinson, Arts Council of England

Chris Roderick, DIAL Tendring

Alan Roulstone, University of Sunderland

Vivien Runnels

Bob Sapey, University of Central Lancashire

Sara Savitch-Lee, Adult Dyslexia Society

Rachel Scott, Richmond Fellowship

S.A. Scott, Garden Craft Products

Susan Scott-Parker, Employers Forum on Disability

Donald Schloss, Adult Dyslexia Organisation

George Shand, Into Work

Surinder Sharma, Littlewoods Organisation

Linda Shaw, Somerset County Council

Mary Shek, Cystic Fibrosis Society

Geoff Shepherd, The Sainsbury Centre

Sickle Cell Society

Ken Simons, Norah Fry Research Centre

Brian Simpson, Working Life Project

Sandy Slack

Amy Small, Directions Plus

Bev Smith, Durham Community Health Trust

S.E. Smith

Nik Standing

John Stanier

Marian Stead, South Tyneside Coalition of the Disabled

A.D. Stevenson, South Lanarkshire Economic Development

Angela Talbot-White, ACENVO

David Tares

Beth Tegg, Comic Relief

Jeannette Thomas, Arts Disability Wales

Adrian Thompson

Gill Thompson

Judith Thurgood

Christine Tillsley, Royal National Institute for the Blind

Brian Tobin, West Wales Training and Enterprise Council

Malcolm Turloy, Middlesborough Borough Council

Bob Twitchin

Diana Twitchin

H. de Vere, DISCASS

Linda Ward, Joseph Rowntree Foundation

Jeff Ware, Rushmoor Voluntary Service

Andrea Wayman, Elite Self Employment Agency

Jean Weaver, East Lancs. Into Employment

Vanessa Webb, Wales Council for the Blind

Stuart Whant, ASPIRE

Derek Wheel, Sabre

Andrea Whittaker, King's Fund

Barbara Williams, Groundwork St Helens

Debbie Williams, Headway Cardiff

John Willmore

Shelley Willson, Lancaster University

Nick Winch, Colchester Gay Switchboard

Gill Winfield, ASBAH (Association for Spina Bifida and Hydrocephalus)

Alys Young, University of Salford

Gerry Zarb, Policy Studies Institute